Digital Social Mind

John Bolender

imprint-academic.com

Copyright © John Bolender, 2011

The moral rights of the author have been asserted.
No part of this publication may be reproduced in any form
without permission, except for the quotation of brief passages
in criticism and discussion.

Published in the UK by
Imprint Academic, PO Box 200, Exeter EX5 5YX, UK

Published in the USA by
Imprint Academic, Philosophy Documentation Center
PO Box 7147, Charlottesville, VA 22906-7147, USA

ISBN 978184540 197 9

A CIP catalogue record for this book is available from the
British Library and US Library of Congress

Contents

	List of Abbreviations	v
	Introduction	vii
	Gratitude	ix
1	Particles and Maps	1
2	Kinds of Idealisation	25
3	Building the Infinite	42
4	Universal Moral Grammar	50
5	Computer Wars	57
6	Beyond the Infinite	68
	Envoy	80
	Glossary	82
	Bibliography	89

List of Abbreviations

AR	Authority Ranking
CS	Communal Sharing
EM	Equality Matching
MP	Market Pricing
NL	Natural Language
RMT	Relational Models Theory
SPG	Social Pattern Generator
UMG	Universal Moral Grammar

Introduction

Language exhibits systematicity. The ability to generate a sentence virtually guarantees the ability to generate another sentence semantically close to the first. For example, one's ability to generate *Plato admired Socrates* practically guarantees the ability to generate *Socrates admired Plato*. Systematicity illustrates the particulate and combinatorial nature of language, that a sentence consists of constituents, particles, which can be combined in more than one manner.

One also finds systematicity in social-relational cognition. One's ability to conceive of a certain type of social structure greatly probabilifies one's ability to conceive of a rearrangement of that structure. The ability to mentally represent a group of equals embedded in a superordinate authoritarian structure, means that one can almost certainly represent an authorit- arian structure embedded in a superordinate structure of equality. One could imagine, for example, a ranking of departments in a corporation, one department giving orders to any department lower than itself. Within each department, however, members could still function and interact as perfect equals. One can also imagine the reverse: a set of families with a paternalistic hierarchical arrangement within each family, with the families themselves interacting as perfect equals. This suggests that particles are combined to form more complex mental representations in social-relational cognition too.

Language also exhibits productivity, more specifically digital infinity (Chomsky, 2000a; 2000b). A phrase, such as a sentence, consists of constituents which can be counted using natural numbers. To put it roughly (very roughly),

Plato admired Socrates contains three words. This is the digital aspect of language. Its infinity results from the ability to embed a phrase within a phrase with no principled upper limit. For example, one can embed *Plato admired Socrates* in the frame *I believe that…* to get *I believe that Plato admired Socrates*. This result can be embedded in the same frame to yield *I believe that I believe that Plato admired Socrates*, and so on. Like systematicity, productivity also suggests the combination of objects to form more complex structures.

One also finds digital infinity in social-relational cognition. In fact, it is much of the burden of this book to show that it is digitally infinite. Namely, one can conceive of a social structure embedded within a social structure embedded within a social structure, etc., with no principled bound on the number of embeddings. Given its systematicity and productivity, it is very plausible that social-relational cognition uses a computational procedure. That is, it uses a combinatorial procedure that respects semantic relations. What exactly that means will be spelled out in later pages.

In an earlier book, *The Self-Organizing Social Mind* (2010), I focused mainly on dynamical processes in social-relational cognition. Dynamicist approaches to cognition are often contrasted with computational approaches, as will be discussed later. One could even get the false impression from the literature that the two are incompatible, that hybridisation is not possible. My claim has been that the formal properties of the basic units of social-relational cognition strongly suggest that these basic units result from dynamical processes. They are not to be understood computationally. However, there is more to social-relational cognition than its basic units, for there is also complex social-relational cognition. When one turns to the latter, one finds mental representations that exhibit systematicity and digital infinity; that is, one finds something strongly suggestive of digital computation. The result is a hybrid view of social-relational cognition, a *computational* system acting upon *dynamically* produced atoms. While in *The Self-Organizing Social Mind* I mainly discussed the dynamical component, in this book, I aim to give the computational part more of its due. In fact, I propose a universal generative grammar for social-relational cognition. That grammar, in turn, evidently interacts with analogue systems to produce particular social-relational grammars. The final picture includes dynamical self-organisation, digital computation and analogue processes. Although novel in some ways, the picture is also classic faculty psychology: different mental powers operate according to different principles whilst also interfacing to produce complex interactions.

Gratitude

For helpful discussions, I thank Şinasi Arslan, Enis Doko, Cem Kamözüt and Cemil Kerimoğlu. For feedback on a very early draft, I thank two anonymous referees assisting Imprint Academic. A draft of Chapter Two was read by members of the RMT Discussion Group including Rodrigo Brito, Fabio Fasoli, Ana Louceiro, Mara Mazzurega, Maria Paolo Palladino, Thomas Schubert, Maciek Sekerdej and Sven Waldzus. Very useful discussion ensued, and I thank everyone. Umut Baysan and David Pierce read later drafts of the manuscript and provided very helpful comments. Email exchanges with Noam Chomsky, Terence Langendoen and Paul Postal were invaluable in preparing Chapter Six. Selma Aydın supplied important technical assistance. I owe a special debt of gratitude to Anthony Freeman who suggested that I write this book in the first place. The author remains solely responsible for remaining deficiencies.

Chapter One

Particles and Maps

Any completed science has basic principles. Simply arriving at plausible basic principles is an accomplishment; devising means for testing naturally comes later. Clues as to basic principles for a science of social- relational cognition can be found in noticing formal properties of the mental models used in structuring social relationships. Fairly simple and straightforward observations of social relations indicate some of these formal properties. One observes variety, for example.

The forms of human social interaction display wide variety, not only across cultures but within them. In the course of one's day, one meets with many remarkably different social expectations. Social interactions at home, at work, at a commencement ceremony, at the pub, in the train are all markedly different. If one were to travel across different societies, the differences would multiply. What produces wide variety? The biologist Ronald Fisher noted that the wide variety of biological species suggests that inheritance depends upon the combination of objects to form novel structures, such that an object does not lose its identity or essentially change when combined with another. This stands in contrast to the blending of unstructured substances (Fisher, 1958, Ch. 1). Blending averages out differences. If the folk view were correct, namely that the child resembles the parents because the child contains a mixture of mother and father's blood, then sexual reproduction would tend toward sameness. But this is not what is found in evolutionary branching. In producing great variety, natural selection must operate upon a system that combines units to form structures, a particulate system.

Consider the immune system. The number of protein-coding genes in the human genome is estimated at between 20,000 and 25,000 (International Human Genome Sequencing Consortium, 2001; 2004). Since the human body can synthesise more than 100 million antibody proteins, there can't be a gene for each antibody. To be responsive to the vast range of potential infections, the immune system must be particulate (Janeway, 1993). The particulate nature of technology also plays a role in its widely diverse evolutionary branching. If you open a jet engine, you find components. If you were to open certain machines that predated the jet engine, you would find many of the same components (Arthur, 2009, pp. 18f). For example, compressors are found in jet engines, and were also found earlier in industrial blower units. If technology were a blending system, it would not exhibit such great diversity and growth.William Abler extended Fisher's reasoning to language, the range and variety of sentences being due to there being basic particles of language which can be combined without limit to form new sentences (1989; cf. Pinker, 1995, pp. 75f).

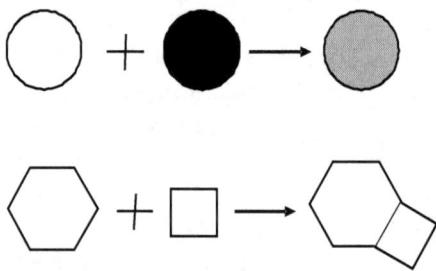

Figure 1

The above sequences, from Abler (1989, p. 2), contrast blending systems and particulate systems. Both types of system produce novelty. The upper tier illustrates how novelty in a blending system is an averaging of inputs. As a result, repeated blending among a set of objects results in greater uniformity. Ironically, it is the sort of novelty that diminishes variety. The lower tier shows how combination in a particulate system normally results in novelty which is strikingly different from the original objects. Repeated combination of objects will not necessarily lead to greater uniformity. In many cases of particulate combination, it results in greater variety.

The wide variety of forms of human social interaction strongly suggests that there is a system in interpersonal cognition for combining objects into complex structures, analogous to the combination of atoms to form molecules or alleles to form a genotype. In linguistics, elementary units, which enter into combination, have sometimes been called 'primes' (Chomsky, 1975, p. 6). The great variety of social structures suggests that there are primes in social-relational cognition as well.

Blending systems are a subclass of analogue systems. In an analogue system, novelty results from changing position in a continuous space. The result of blending white paint and red paint can be represented as a point on a finite one-dimensional space, a bounded line. Purely red paint corresponds to one end of the line. Purely white paint corresponds to the other end. Different proportions of blending correspond to different shades of pink; they also correspond to in-between points on the line. The transition from, say, pure red to some particular shade of pink is a kind of novelty. It can be represented as a change in position on the line. Blending three colours of paint can be represented using a two-dimensional space. Novelty would then correspond to change of position within a triangle. Blending four paints would correspond to a three-dimensional space. And so on.

Some animal communication systems are analogue, including some human systems of communication. One can raise one's voice to communicate degree of anger, conveying a new degree of anger by changing the volume of one's voice. One is here moving to a new position within the one-dimensional space of loudness. W.H. Thorpe notes that the European robin trills more or less quickly to reflect its degree of willingness to defend its territory (cited in Chomsky, 2006, pp. 59f). A change of position within the one-dimensional space of trilling frequency conveys new information. The waggle dance of the honeybee is analogue as well. The degree of the waggling line of the bee's dance, in relation to the perpendicular, indicates the angle of the direction to food or water in relation to the sun. Change in angle, within this two-dimensional space, corresponds to new information (Frisch, 1967).

David Braddon-Mitchell and Frank Jackson have proposed what they call 'the map story' of the mind (2007), an attempt to understand thought processes and mental representation in terms of inner mental maps. These maps constitute an analogue system or group of such systems. On a mappish approach, mental representations are continuous, not digital. Being continuous, a map contains, at least in principle, infinitely many points: 'Passages of prose have minimum representational units, maps do not' (Braddon-Mitchell and Jackson, 2007, p. 181). Since each point represents something, a map stores, in principle, an infinite quantity of information. Hence, a map cannot represent any information without representing a lot of information, as Braddon-Mitchell and Jackson point out. The map story is virtually synonymous with the view that there are analogue mental processes, the spaces of analogue thought systems being maps in Braddon-Mitchell and Jackson's sense.

There are two sources of novelty in such a system. The indicator of a thing's location on a map, the pointer, can move. The other source of novelty is that the map itself can deform into a new map or a different version of the same map. But, if one maintains a purely mappish view of thought, this latter source of change turns out to be a special case of the former. A map deforms by itself changing location within a space of possible maps; the map itself moves within a second-order map.

Purely analogue systems are not good explanations of variety, hence are not good explanations of social variety. Simply changing position within defined limits is not a source of interesting variation. Changing position in multiple spaces simultaneously could be a source of interesting variation, but this would be a kind of particulate system, each space serving as a particle. Consider a screen composed of pixels each of which can change in hue along a continuous dimension. Each such pixel is an analogue system, but the combination of pixels is particulate. Mere change of position may seem to be a source of interesting variation if the map itself has a lot of variety built into it, but the variety had to get there somehow. Self-organisation is not the answer, unless the self-organisation itself acts upon primes. Otherwise, self-organisation only produces relatively simple forms, such as tornadoes and Chladni patterns.[1]

Human social structures exhibit much complex design. Plausibly, a particulate system is at least one factor in how humans produce a wide variety of social structures. This leaves open the possibility, however, that analogue and particulate systems are combined in interpersonal cognition.[2] It is important to bear in mind that the mind is not a single faculty, not a single power but, rather, a collection of interacting powers. So the map story could be part of the bigger story. In fact, some analogue approach or other evidently is part of the bigger story, as will be discussed later. The other part is a story about primes and their combination.

What are the primes of interpersonal cognition? Alan Page Fiske's Relational Models Theory (RMT) is the most plausible and scientifically corroborated answer yet to this question (Fiske, 1991; Haslam, 2004a). According to RMT, four basic mental models, universal for the species, are applied to all social relations. This is not to say that only four models are used in social-relational cognition, but that all such models can be analysed into these four. For Fiske, 'each elementary model is a motivated schema *for* constituting social relationships (a guide, plan, or recipe), and a model *of* what is happening in social relationships (that is, a model for understanding, a model that gives meaning to action)' (1991, p. 385). In other words, a model both motivates and brings understanding.

The basic models are as follows:

---

[1] I do not mean to deny that maps can self-organise (cf. Kohonen, 2001). My point is that self-organisation alone is not a source of complex novelty unless it takes a particulate form.
[2] In fairness to Braddon-Mitchell and Jackson, they do mention the possibility of a particulate language of thought and an analogue map system working together (2007, p. 182), but devote only one sentence to the matter.

Communal Sharing (CS): This 'is a relationship of equivalence, in which all the people in some bounded group are considered the same for the social purposes in question' (Fiske *et al.*, 1991, p. 657). All members are seen as sharing a common substance, such as blood, and are not differentiated. Group needs trump individual needs; but because one identifies with the group, this is not perceived as altruism. Nationalism, romantic love, racism and indiscriminate killing of anyone outside of the group in retaliation for an attack upon the group are forms of CS. Decision making structured by CS works by consensus and seeks unanimity. In moral judgments, CS motivates the view that people should share with other group members. 'In transactions, the group pools resources and operates on the principle, What's mine is yours' (Fiske *et al.*, 1991, p. 657).

Authority Ranking (AR): This model structures social interaction with respect to ordered differences, with people or groups standing in a linear hierarchy. It is thus a relationship of inequality. Subordinates are expected to respect and obey, and superiors enjoy greater prestige whilst also having duties of protection and care for their inferiors. Superiors receive greater social benefits, and outline social norms. 'Initiative often rests with the highest ranking person or people in a social relationship, and authority typically confers certain related prerogatives involving choice and preference' (Fiske, 1991, p. 14). Examples include military rankings, ethnic rankings, ancestor worship and monotheism.

Equality Matching (EM) relationships involve maintaining or restoring balance or one-to-one correspondence. 'Shares of a given substance, turns, or things given in return for earlier help should balance or match... precisely. In the same sense, persons in an equality matching relationship are treated as distinct but interchangeable with each other' (Fiske, 1990, p. 185). Note that this last feature differs from CS in which individuals are not treated as distinct from each other. Examples of EM include equal time, equal team size and rules for taking turns; also restitution in kind, and equivalent contributions.

Proportion is the core concept of **Market Pricing** (MP). Interactions are conceived in terms of rates or ratios such as prices, wages, interest, rents, tithes, or cost-benefit analyses. Utilitarian principles, including 'the greatest happiness for the greatest number', are structured by MP. 'People using this model make decisions according to rational calculations of cost and benefit or supply and demand, as when the market determines what commodities are produced, where, how, and by whom' (Fiske *et al.*, 1991, p. 657). MP does not, however, always involve maximisation or minimisation; determining the right price for a commodity, for example, does not always involve maximising profit or minimising loss. MP also informs judgments of the right proportion for reward or punishment.

On RMT, individuals use these models to understand, anticipate, guide and respond to social interactions. This includes large-scale social structures (states, economies) as well as seemingly trivial mundane interactions (buying coffee in a café). The principle of one-person-one-vote is structured by EM, but so is the custom of waiting in line at the post office. The relation between emperor and subject is informed by AR, but so is the custom of reserving coffee for grown-ups. Whenever people choose to emphasise something they have in common, this is CS. CS structures the intense patriotism which could cause one to give up one's life for one's homeland. But it also structures two people sharing a snack, at least when no tabs are kept as to how much each one eats. MP structures the economics of the market place. It also structures the decision of a parent in deciding the right amount of reward to give their child for some good deed. The presence of the four models across diverse societies is no less remarkable than their ubiquity in both grand and minute social relations.

The last example also illustrates how models can be combined (Fiske, 1991, Ch. 7). Even though the parent's decision is structured by MP, the parent's right to make the decision illustrates AR. AR and MP are combined in this case. Combination of models is very common. The prerogative of grown-ups to drink coffee at the dinner table is AR, but the sharing of food during the same meal is CS. The combinatorial property of the models is largely what this book is about. This property suggests that relational cognition is a particulate system in which simple mental symbols are combined to yield complex ones. It suggests that, in thinking about social interactions which exhibit even very modest degrees of complexity, a computational operation is at work.

The models, however, are not applied to all human interaction. When a model is not applied to an interaction between persons, this is known as the null relation (Fiske, 1991).

> Humans who don't apply any of these moral-relational frameworks can be callously cruel to others, treating other people as if they were objects like rocks, trees, or insects—merely means or impediments to material ends. Sociopaths do this, but so do normal people under extreme conditions: when bullets are flying you may duck behind a rock, a tree, a dead body, or a living body. Normal people also treat strangers like this when their culture does not offer paradigms for applying relational models to out-groups. (Fiske and Ehrenhalt, n.d., p. 11)

The null relation can superficially resemble Authority Ranking. The point is made vividly clear in a passage by Bertrand Russell. Writing in 1938, Russell remarked that:

> Imagine a scientific government which, from fear of assassination, lives always in aeroplanes, except for occasional descents on to landing stages on the summits of high towers or rafts on the sea. Is it likely that such a government will have any profound concern for the happiness of its subjects? Is it not, on the contrary, practically certain that it will view them, when all goes well, in the impersonal manner in which it view sits machines, but that, when anything happens to suggest that after all they are not machines, it will feel the cold rage of men whose axioms are questioned by underlings, and will exterminate resistance in whatever manner involves least trouble? (Russell, 1996, p. 20)

There are indicators here that this is not genuinely Authority Ranking. One is the 'scientific government's' having no sense of pastoral obligation to those under its control. Another is its having no expectation that those under its control would admire or feel any respect for it. Of course, in AR relationships, admiration and respect can be absent. But there is always the feeling that they are supposed to be there, and hence a sense of irony when they are not. In the nightmare scenario described by Russell, by contrast, a lack of respect and admiration would seem perfectly natural and unremarkable. Intuitively, the attitude of such a government toward the relationship, and the attitudes of those under its control, are more akin to the respective attitudes of psychopath and victim than to the normal attitudes of, say, king and subject.

In RMT, social cognition is primarily thinking about relations among persons or groups of persons. This stands in contrast to the more familiar definition of social cognition, namely perception or interpretation of another person. Gordon Moskowitz, for example, equates social cognition with 'interpersonal perception', and notes that 'the main concern of this area of investigation has not varied – analyzing processes of attribution. An *attribution* is the end result of a process of classifying and explaining behavior in order to arrive at a decision regarding the reason or cause for the observed behavior' (2004, p. 3). Similarly, social cognition has been defined as 'how people think about people' (Wegner and Wallacher, 1977, p. viii), and as 'the process of understanding or making sense of people' (Worchel *et al.*, 1989, p. 50). Something should be said to justify the RMT approach with its emphasis on the interpretation of relationships rather than individual persons, so let us turn to matters of empirical corroboration.

To test RMT, Fiske and colleagues performed studies examining accidental name substitution as a means of exploring the nature of person perception (Fiske *et al.*, 1991). The results showed the relational models to be better predictors of such mistakes than other ways of categorising people, such as personality, ethnicity and age. Only gender was a better predictor than the models. This result indicates that person perception, the classic conception of social cognition, turns out to be fundamentally thinking about relations. Specifically, it is fundamentally application of the basic relational models of RMT. Person memory errors, in which one wrongly remembers with whom one did something, and misdirected actions, in which one performs an action with a person other than the one intended, were also studied. Fiske and his colleagues predicted that the relational models would generally predict such mistakes (Fiske et al., 1991).

To avoid cultural bias, four of the nine studies were performed on non-Westerners: Koreans, Liberians, Bengalis and Chinese (Fiske, 1993). The results were that, with the exception of gender, the four relational models better predicted these errors than did other perceived characteristics. Deliberate substitutions were also tested, e.g. changing one's mind about the person with whom one meant to perform an activity (Fiske and Haslam, 1997). The results here too supported RMT. Also note that RMT was first devised to account for relational cognition among the Moose of Burkina Faso (Fiske, 1990; 1991). In other words, RMT originated in anthropological work concerning a non-Western people.

In another study (Haslam and Fiske, 1992) subjects listed at least forty people, by name or by description, with whom they had had any social interaction at any time. Two lists of twenty were then created randomly from this list. For one of the shorter lists, subjects assigned a number to each pair of names indicating degree of similarity in interpersonal relationship to the subject. For the other list, subjects sorted descriptors into groups according to similarity of relationship. Each subject sorted descriptors into groups of six and then into groups of four and lastly into two groups. A week later, subjects were informed of the RMT categories and then sorted all forty names accordingly. The second-session results were used to predict how well the various theoretical classifications predict subjects' classifications in the first session. The relational-models typology better predicted the sortings than other sociological and psychological hypotheses.

A further study showed that abnormal over- and under-reliance on one or more of the models coincides with personality disorder (Haslam *et al.*, 2002). In fact, the personality disorders can be more effectively analysed in RMT terms rather than the more familiar circumplex measure (Leary, 1957; Wiggins, 1979). '[S]everal [personality disorders] that do project onto the circumplex have very similar locations, although they are clinically quite distinct. For instance, narcissistic and paranoid [personality disorders] share similar locations [on the circumplex], as do schizoid and avoidant [personality disorders]' (Haslam *et al.*, 2002, p. 20). Consider the first example. Haslam and his colleagues discovered in a controlled study that those with narcissistic personality tend to have a high need for AR, specifically the desire to recognise oneself as occupying the high-status end of the hierarchy in social interactions. Desire and perception, however, are two different things, and the narcissist's perception of social interactions is a bit different from what is desired. In addition to over- perceiving AR, the narcissist tends also to under-perceive EM. So a narcissist will see no need to act in an egalitarian way, even when others expect equal treatment. Paranoid personality, by contrast, was found to coincide with a strong need for MP. In other words, the paranoid person feels the need to rely on risk assessment and cost-benefit thinking. In his perceptions of social interactions, the paranoid person tends to discern AR relations more than normal, and fails to perceive interactions as CS relations when a normal person would. So the paranoid is far more lacking in sympathy than the narcissist. From an RMT perspective, these two personalities can be distinguished. By contrast, using the more conventional interpersonal circle, they would both be lumped together as 'low-solidarity/ high-status', i.e. each is a disagreeable extravert (Paulhus, 2001; see also Haslam, 2004b).[3]

These studies show that the relational models enter into person perception. This, in turn, shows that the mainstream conception of social cognition presupposes interpersonal cognition. RMT captures social cognition on a more fundamental level than does the standard conception of social

---

[3] For more details about controlled evidence for RMT, see (Haslam, 2004c).

cognition. Social cognition is thinking about relationships, even if one defines 'social cognition' as person perception. I will use the term 'relational cognition' to refer to cognition structured by the relational-models framework, so as to avoid confusion. But the term 'social cognition' would, strictly speaking, be appropriate, since the relational models crucially enter into social cognition even given its most conventional characterisation.

Part of the complexity of social life is due to the embedding of one instance of a relational model within another instance of a model (Fiske, 1991, pp. 150f). This embedding is the particulate component of relational cognition. The point was briefly illustrated earlier in discussing the case of the parent deciding how best to reward their child: a combination of AR and MP. It is also possible to embed a model of a certain type within a model of the same type such as a ranking of individuals within each social unit with the social units themselves ranked. This would be an instance of AR embedded in another instance of AR. Fiske describes examples that extend well beyond a single embedding, such as the following example involving Market Pricing:

> In many sophisticated large-scale markets, there are… futures markets in which traders buy, sell, and maintain a market in contracts to buy or sell various commodities at various times in the future…
>
> [P]eople may buy and sell whole markets. A corporation may buy a sports or food franchise, which is the right to sell a given product to individual consumers in a given market. Franchises for the entrepreneurial rights to sell a given kind of commodity (hamburgers, baseball games, or computers) are exchanged in a market mode, and on a larger scale individuals and companies bid to buy other companies in 'takeovers.' This is trade in trade, a market in markets. (Fiske, 1991, pp. 154–55)

In other words, MP relations can themselves be bought and sold for the right price, a superordinate use of MP.

An instance of EM can also be embedded in another instance of EM. One illustration of this is Anton Pannekoek's conception of council communism (2003). In Pannekoek's system, the workplace is organised via EM.

'The great task of the workers is the organisation of production on a new basis. It has to begin with the organisation within the shop... Collaboration of equal companions replaces the command of masters and the obedience of servants' (Pannekoek, 2003, p. 19). A council of workers democratically decides upon its interests and chooses a delegate to represent them in a superordinate council also structured by EM. Measures are taken to prevent an AR relation between delegate and constituents: 'The delegates constituting them have been sent by sectional assemblies with special instructions; they return to these assemblies to report on the discussion and its result...' (*ibid.*, p. 21). Delegates are quickly rotated. The choice of delegate will sometimes reflect the nature of the council's immediate concern (*ibid.*, p. 24). They can be withdrawn at any time if they do not represent the interests of the subordinate council they represent. This recursion is indefinite, at least in principle. A superordinate council elects a delegate to represent them in an even more superordinate council. And so on. Each such structure is finite, since it is capped by a supreme council. So the totality of conceivable council communist societies is infinite.

Recursive use of AR is easy to imagine, being simply the hierarchical ranking of hierarchical rankings. There is evidence that hamadryas baboons mentally represent recursive AR rankings with regard to their own social structures (Bergman *et al.*, 2003).

Fiske gives examples of instances of CS embedded in superordinate instances of CS as found among the Moose of Burkina Faso. Moose society consists of units organised according to CS, each unit known as *buudu*. On the most subordinate level, a *buudu* is a polygamous family known as *zaka*. Members of a *zaka* live together, eat together, and cultivate the land together, sharing living space, food, and work. A number of *zakas* belong to the same sublineage. A number of sublineages belong to the same lineage. A number of lineages form a superordinate *buudu* protected by a common totem. A number of such *buudus* constitute an ethnic subgroup, a number of which constitute the Moose as a people.

'Each represents – in ever decreasing intensity and a more limited range of domains as they expand – a Communal Sharing relationship. So the innermost group shares most of their labor and food, while intermediate groups share food and labor only occasionally...' (Fiske, 1991, p. 51). One may question whether this recursion really is indefinite. After all, wouldn't the fact that CS bonds grow weaker on each level force termination at a point that could perhaps even be predicted? It is important to bear in mind, however, that practical limitations constraining, say, food sharing do not apply here. The focus of this book is on mental representation *viz.* something internal and psychological, not on how the models are externalised. Still, one might insist that the weakening of emotional bonds as one ascends levels is psychological. But this should be considered as a performance limitation rather than a reflection of one's knowledge of how to mentally embed one model in another. Performance limitations will soon be discussed at length.

Instances of different models can also be combined to form complex social structures. I noted earlier that council communism illustrates recursive EM, but the sort of society envisioned by Pannekoek would involve even more complex combinations of models than that. The recursively structured arrangement of councils would consist of workers only. Rentiers and stockholders would not be part of these democratic structures, hence a kind of dictatorship of the proletariat would initially be in force (Pannekoek, 2003, p. 48). The recursively structured councils would themselves be bound together by an overarching ethos of CS. Pannekoek speaks of 'a humanity that has bound itself consciously by strong ties of brotherhood into a working community controlling its own life' (*ibid.*, p. 52). Hence, at least in the early days of council communism, as anticipated by Pannekoek, recursively embedded EM structures would themselves be embedded in an overarching CS structure. In the early stages at least, the former rentiers and stockholders would not be workers, and so evidently would not enjoy this bond. The remaining bourgeoisie would form another social group standing in a lower-ranking AR relation to that

CS structure. The entire structure would be AR with at least one component of the AR relation structured by CS. That CS component, in turn, would be internally structured by multiple instances of hierarchically embedded EM structures. With the anticipated disappearance of the bourgeoisie, the dominant model would be CS with recursively structured EM constituents.

Even in small-scale social structures, one finds complexity resulting from the embedding of models. A marriage, to use one of Fiske's examples (1991, pp. 156–57), could easily consist of AR with respect to some specific issue (as in a Japanese wife's authority over financial matters in the household). The very same marriage could also incorporate domains structured by CS, such as the more romantic moments. The domain of cooking and washing dishes could be structured by EM, specfically turn taking. A marriage could even incorporate MP, if one spouse is an employee of the other. These relations may not all be mentally represented simultaneously, but the point is that they could be. Otherwise you would not be able to reflect upon the complex nature of such a marriage, and you just did. The same point applies to large societies. One may not always be thinking about the complex nature of a given society. But one could do so. Otherwise, you would not be able to imagine the sort of society described by Pannekoek.

Hence, not all relational models are elementary, as there are also compound models which result from embedding. We thus recognise RMT to describe a particulate system. The vast range of dramatically contrasting social structures is no surprise, given that there are social primes and a means to use embedding to generate compound representations from them.

A model must be interpreted by various mental faculties in order to be applied to social situations, whether in action or thought. I use the word 'semantic' to mean such interpretation. There is a sense in which the semantics of a model is part of the model, a relational model being a union of two aspects, one formal and the other semantic. Among the formal properties of the models are their strong resemblance to the four scale types of classic measurement theory.[4] For discussion, see Fiske (1991), Bolender (2010). Other formal properties are due to a combinatorial operation, to be discussed later.

The distinction between the formal and the semantic is partly reflected in Fiske's distinction between mods and preos.

> These are the four fundamental, innate, human relational proclivities. To signify that they are cognitively modular but modifiable modes of interacting, I call them 'mods.' However, these open-ended generative potentials are insufficient in themselves to determine action or evaluation, or permit coordination. In order to use these mods to act or to interpret others' action, people need socially transmitted prototypes, precedents, and principles that complete the mods, specifying how when and with respect to whom the mods apply. I use the term 'preo' to signify the class of paradigms, parameters, precepts, prescriptions, propositions, and proscriptions that can be conjoined with mods. A mod must be conjoined with a preo that complements it to generate a specific cultural coordination device. (Fiske, 2004, pp. 3–4)

> These mods are relational structures that can be implemented in innumerable ways. Hence a mod requires cultural complements that complete it, a set of *preos*. Preos are cultural prototypes, precedents, precepts, or principles that orient the mod by indicating with whom, what, when, where, and how it is implemented in any specific instance. Preos can be folk tales, proverbs, holy books, sermons, children's stories, movies or television shows, admonishments or punishments experienced or observed, explanations, or experiences of interaction that the child is able to use to orient her mods. The preos are what is culturally transmitted that the child must detect and learn. (Fiske, forthcoming)

There is some ambiguity in Fiske's definition of 'mod'. The first two sentences of the 2004 quote imply that all mods are elementary. The third sentence identifies them as 'generative potentials', raising the question of whether mods can be used to generate more complex representations. The second

---

[4] I use 'syntactic' to mean combinatorial, and so need a broader term, 'formal', to include non-semantic properties that are not combinatorial. A prime's resemblance to a measurement scale is thus formal but not syntactic.

quote (forthcoming) simply refers to a mod as the structural aspect of a model. Given that models can be compound, and given that compounding is structural, then there can also be compound mods. There seem to be two senses of 'mod', one narrow referring to elementary objects only and the other broader. I use 'mod' in the broader sense, a mod thus being either elementary or compound.

But the mod/preo distinction, even thus clarified, does not precisely map onto the formal/semantic distinction. Although, by Fiske's definition, preos are wholly learned, elsewhere he discusses semantic elements of models not all of which are so obviously learned (1991). To take one example among many, CS and AR differ in the manner in which they are characteristically externalised. CS is characteristically externalised by touching and movement in rhythmic unison. AR is characteristically externalised using ordered arrays (e.g. the leader coming first, the first deputy arriving second, etc.) and size differences (e.g. the emperor's chair being the largest, etc.) CS and AR also differ in terms of attitudes toward time. The former conceives temporal relations as eternal and stresses the perpetuation of tradition by replicating the past. AR conceives time as marking status either in terms of sequence or duration. While these are clearly semantic matters, it is not clear that they are learned. Since this book focuses on the formal properties of models, it is useful to have terminology for distinguishing the formal features of models from their features of interpretation, learned or not. I propose for purposes of this book to alter the definitions of 'mod' and 'preo' slightly. Let 'mod' mean the formal properties of a given model. Let 'preo' refer to its semantic properties whether innate or learned.

Most cultural anthropology and most social psychology focus on preos. One might even say that cultural anthropology does so by definition. Abstracting out preos to focus on mods results in a scientific field that would seem alien to many anthropologists and social psychologists. But, if RMT is correct, mods constitute the core of what is externalised as interpersonal relations. Mods would thus be relevant to nearly everything studied in cultural anthropology. Even if mods stand outside the *definition* of cultural anthropology, they are tightly causally linked to its subject matter and should be of interest to cultural anthropologists for that reason. I suggest that anthropologists and social psychologists accustom themselves to the more formal and abstract observations that would typify a science of mods. Otherwise, there is a danger that these disciplines will confine themselves to highly complex peripheral contributions to relational cognition that are less theoretically dissectable. It is the relatively simple core of relational cognition which may most easily lend itself to a deep understanding.

Reflecting on the formal properties of the elementary mods provides clues as to how they come into being in the brain-mind (Bolender, 2007a; 2008; 2010). Reflecting on formal properties of compound mods also provides clues as to their principles of construction. One such property evidently is indefinite recursion, i.e. digital infinity. A compound mod is digital in the sense that it consists of constituent mods which can be counted using natural numbers. One doesn't have a complex mod consisting of four and a half instances of elementary mods. Compound mods are infinite in the sense that there are potentially infinitely many of them due to their recursive embedding. In terms of compounding, there is no greatest mod, suggesting that complex mods result from a constructive operation.

An operation is constructive if, and only if, it is performed on a finite number of objects in a finite number of steps yielding a set of objects. The reason to think that language employs a constructive operation is that it exhibits digital infinity.

> An elementary fact about the language faculty is that it is a system of discrete infinity. Any such system is based on a primitive operation that takes n objects already constructed, and constructs from them a new object: in the simplest case, the set of these n objects. Call that operation Merge. Either Merge or some equivalent is a minimal requirement. With Merge available, we instantly have an unbounded system of hierarchically structured expressions. (Chomsky, 2005, p. 11)

Consider an example of Merge in language. In parsing the phrase *to need some help*, one merges *help* with the determiner *some* to yield a determiner phrase. The determiner phrase is merged with *need* to form a verb phrase which is merged with *to* yielding an infinitive phrase. The result is a structure exhibiting multiple embeddings.

[infinitive phrase*to* [verb phrase*need* [determiner phrase*some* [noun*help*]]]]

Mere repetition does not yield digital infinity. The repetitive flashing of a firefly, while digital, is not infinite. The same signal is simply repeated. This being mere repetition of a single signal means that the firefly's number is 1, not an infinite number. With set construction, it's a different story. Consider a form of Merge which takes {X} as input and produces {Y, {X}} as output, for any X and any Y. For example:

$$\{\alpha\},$$
$$\{\alpha, \{\alpha\}\},$$
$$\{\alpha, \{\alpha, \{\alpha\}\}\},$$
and so on.

$\{a, \{a, \{a\}\}\}$ is a new object, not merely repetition of $\{a\}$. Unlike mere repetition, set construction is productive.[5]

Here we see what is wrong with David Hume's psychology (Fodor, 2003, pp. 90f). For Hume, the primes of thought are copies of sense impressions; we form new ideas by associating these primes. That is, Hume thought that from the primes α and β, one could associate the two to form a new idea consisting of both, namely α β. But what exactly is α β? Given that association is a tendency to have one idea followed by another, mere association does not yield a compound object; it just yields α followed by β. We do not have here a third object but just the original two. Association of ideas does not explain how we form new thoughts that are not merely copies of sense impressions. A Humean might

---

[5] I was confused about this in my article (2007b, p. 385) in which I opined that *hierarchially structured* digital infinity requires Merge. But matters are simpler. The digitally infinite use of finite means *as such* requires Merge.

insist that α and β are integrated by association into a new compound object; but in that case, the Humean *is* appealing to Merge. That is, the Humean vacillates between sometimes using 'association' to mean association and, at other times, cheating by using it to mean Merge. When doing the former, the Humean cannot explain the productivity of thought. When doing the latter, the Humean is acknowledging an unlearned generative procedure, something stronger than mere association.

That language is digitally infinite can be defended in more detail. Attaching a finite number to language would be arbitrary. Zellig Harris (1957, pp. 338–39), for example, notes that one cannot set up a reasonable description of a language that implies its being finite. Any attempt to do so would have to place a limit on some recursive operation, such as the number of times that *and* can appear in a sentence. Any such stipulation would be 'highly arbitrary and numerical' (*ibid.*, p. 339). A more explicit formulation of what I take to be the same argument is found in Paul Postal (2003a, pp. 245f) who notes that any attempt to posit a finite bound, m, for sentence length faces two challenges:

> Challenge 1:
> What argues that the bound is m and not $m + 1$?
>
> Challenge 2:
> What argues that the bound is m and not $m - 1$?

Postal goes on to note that 'there is no non-arbitrary way to pick m that justifies it against either a smaller bound or a bigger one' (*ibid.*, p. 246). Postal also observes that one cannot argue for the finitude of language by placing a vague bound on sentence length. Challenges analogous to 1 and 2 above would still apply. An approximate bound is just as arbitrary as a unique bound.

Of course there is some sense in which one could put a non-arbitrary cap on sentence length. The question is whether that sense is relevant to devising a theory of grammar. Consider an example: for any sentence of the form *It is* [adj.] *that* [decl. sent.] there is a corresponding sentence of the form *That* [decl. sent.] *is* [adj.]. Given that *It is upsetting that Mehmet left* is grammatical, then so too is *That Mehmet left is upsetting*. Given that *It is surprising that it is upsetting that Mehmet left*, then *It is suprising that that Mehmet left is upsetting* is also grammatical. Given that *It is suprising that that Mehmet left is upsetting* is grammatical, then *That that Mehmet left is upsetting is surprising* is also grammatical. In similar fashion, *That that that Mehmet left is upsetting is surprising is interesting* is also grammatical, as too is *That that that that Mehmet left is upsetting is surprising is interesting is getting to be tedious*. But if one encountered *That that that that Mehmet left is upsetting is surprising is interesting is getting to be tedious*, without an explanation of how it was constructed, it would seem ungrammatical. Does this mean that there are limits on recursion in language? Given a finite lexicon and limited recursion, is language finite after all?

A similar question would be whether one's knowledge of mathematics is finite. There is a sense in which one's knowledge of mathematics is infinite, since the mathematical operations one knows yield infinitely many results. But there are still limits on what one can do with this knowledge. For example, one may know the rules of multiplication, rules which solve an infinite set of problems, but one may not be able to perform a certain multiplication problem in one's head because it is too complicated. One could do so, however, if one's short-term memory were sufficiently extended. Likewise, one could automatically parse *That that that that Mehmet left is upsetting is surprising is interesting is getting to be tedious* if one's short-term memory were sufficiently boosted. That way, one could keep track of each *that* and link it to the right verb phrase.

In order to better understand what is happening in these cases, Chomsky distinguishes competence from performance (1965). Competence is knowledge, such as the knowledge of how to construct a sentence or solve a mathematical problem. In the case of language, it is taken to be unconscious knowledge; most speakers do not consciously understand how to parse a sentence, but they obviously parse sentences just the same. Performance is the implementation of knowledge. Performance systems are faculties which access competence so as to implement it, e.g. short-term memory (1995, pp. 168–69). Chomsky factors out performance limitations in claiming that language is digitally infinite.

One possible objection is that there may be no pertinent performance limitations here. Maybe our knowledge of the structure of language is simply finite. But there must be a constructive procedure underlying language; otherwise, one would have to memorise every sentence that one can use, and the number of usable sentences is astronomical. Positing a constructive operation is a much simpler hypothesis. In linguistics, the term 'generative' is often used to mean constructive, and so one hears of generative grammar.

Postal's argument for the digital infinity of language can be applied analogously to relational cognition, specifically the system of mods. As such, Postal's two challenges have analogues for anyone denying that the mods are indefinitely recursive.

Digital infinity, broad variety, and systematicity are reasons for positing Merge in relational cognition. Relational Merge turns out to be a digital computational procedure. Computation is an algorithmic process which functions to yield semantically evaluable outputs. The classic model here is the Turing machine, which is further appropriate for the current discussion as it is digital, operating in discrete steps. A Turing machine is only causally sensitive to formal properties of symbols even though it is semantically well behaved, i.e. its outputs yield semantically coherent results. In relational cognition, likewise, Merge only acts upon formal constituents, namely mods, but it yields objects which are semantically interpreted by preonic systems yielding relational models.

Some have argued that uniquely human cognition crucially depends upon digital computation in language, i.e. linguistic Merge. Drawing upon work of Elizabeth Spelke (2003), Cedric Boeckx reviews evidence for five innate specialised mental faculties that humans share with other species: navigation, numerosity, naïve physics, naïve geometry and social cognition (Boeckx, 2010, Ch. 8). Boeckx goes on to review evidence indicating that any uniquely human mental powers in addition to these five draw upon the combinatorial power of language syntax.

Does the digital infinity in relational cognition draw upon the same combinatorial mechanism as language? Will relational Merge turn out to be an application of linguistic Merge? I submit that the matter is not currently clear. But there is some soft evidence that relational cognition exhibits digital infinity independently of language. One source of evidence is the presence of recursively structured CS in dolphins.[6] Another is evidence for recursively structured AR in hamadryas baboons (Bergman *et al.*, 2003). But the evidence is equivocal. Recursion alone does not equal digital infinity. The point can be made by considering some recent experimental work on other species. Timothy Gentner and colleagues found that European starlings can be trained to recognise the recursive pattern [a[ab]b] (2006). But this does not show that starlings are using a generative procedure for pattern recognition, unless one can show that the recursive pattern can be indefinitely expanded. Otherwise, starlings may simply mentally represent a template of the form [x[xy]x] which can be filled in as needed. An analogous point applies to H. Paul Grice's account of semantics in language. For Grice, when a speaker makes an utterance to an audience with the meaning that, say, snow is white, the speaker intends that [the audience recognise that [the speaker wants [the audience to believe that [the speaker thinks that [snow is white]]]]] (1969). Note that we here have four recursions in the speaker's thought. Grice saw no reason to posit indefinitely many recursions. Just four. Like the starling, the human may be using a ready-made template rather than a generative procedure for forming communicative intentions. If so, this would be an example of

---

[6] Male bottlenose dolphins form alliances embedded within alliances (Connor, 2007). Males in such an alliance share females, touch each other, and jump from the water in unison. Sharing, touching, and moving in rhythmic unison are indications of CS (Fiske, 2004). On the other hand, given the great evolutionary distance between dolphins and humans, it is not clear what relevance such recursion might have to human cognition.

definite recursion. This stands in contrast to syntax in human language, for there is no normal length for a sentence.

Among fractals in organic nature, one finds both definite and indefinite recursion. Capillaries, tree branches, leaves and mitochondria are fractal. But they do not exhibit indefinite recursion. For a given species of tree, there is also a normal adult size for the tree and for one of its leaves. These are cases of definite recursion, not digital infinity. Precambrian rangeomorphs exhibited a fractal growth pattern, as we know from exquisitely preserved fossil remains (Narbonne, 2004). But unlike trees and capillaries their fractal growth was indefinite. 'Nearly all animals stop growing when they reach a certain size: not so with these organisms [rangeomorphs]. In these important respects, they resemble fungi rather than animals. Scientists had to conclude that they could not place them with any living types of animal' (O'Donoghue, 2007, p. 37). Here we find indefinite recursion in the biological world. A fungus also exhibits no normal adult size and, like rangeomorphs, fungi have fractal structures. Specifically, fungi exhibit radial growth, expanding outwardly through the branching of threadlike elements. (This is less apparent in mushrooms, because the fractal mycelium is hidden.) Given that there is no normal degree of complexity for a mod, they look more like rangemorphs or fungi. There is no normal 'adult size' for a mental representation of a social structure. This clearly indicates generativity.

Summary

The wide variety of social structures suggests a particulate system is at work in relational cognition. That is, primes are combined in relational cognition to form representations of complex social relations. Evidently, the primes are the elementary mods of relational models theory. (More specifically, they are copies of basic mods, as will be discussed in Chapter Three.) The digital infinity of the mods means that a set-constructive procedure is at work. More specifically, digital computation accounts for the generation of complex mods.

Chapter Two
Kinds of Idealisation

As noted, the argument for language exhibiting digital infinity presupposes the distinction between competence and performance. The distinction, however, does not lack critics:

> The investigation of recursive and augmentative structures in animal cognition is a current minor industry in cognitive science. If this is meant to shed light on the human language capacity, it is arguably quite misguided. Indefinite recursion, or discrete infinity as Chomsky prefers, is not an actual property of human language—no human is capable of indefinite centre-embedding, for example. Only in the light of a radical distinction between competence and performance does this minor industry make any sense at all, and that little sense is undermined by the impossibility of testing animals directly for indefinite recursion. (Evans and Levinson, 2009, p. 482; see also Sampson, 2002, pp. 80f; Boden, 2006, pp. 417–18)

If this is reason for denying that language is indefinitely recursive, it is also reason for denying that relational cognition is indefinitely recursive. Performance limitations prevent anyone's relational cognition from actually exhibiting digital infinity. Clearly, mortality places a finite limit. This is not only a remark about the implementation of a relational model in social life. It is a remark about one's ability to mentally represent indefinitely many mods.

The gist of the criticism seems to be that, since performance limitations are real, anyone factoring them out has lost touch with reality hence devising a kind of fantasy science. If one is to predict as much behaviour of the system as possible, as many factors as possible bearing on behaviour must be factored in. These include performance limitations.

The only exception might be cases in which too many factors result in computational intractability. But, even in those cases, one puts the missing factors back in as soon as a means is acquired for handling the full computational load. Or so the reasoning seems to be. In other words, the question arises whether factoring out performance limitations is legitimate scientific idealisation.

Earlier, we noted Postal's argument for language being indefinitely recursive. Postal also argues *against* the indefinite recursivity of language (2009). He is not contradicting himself. Postal only acknowledges indefinite recursion when language is construed as an abstract object, a thing having no location in space or time. This would be analogous to viewing the mods as purely abstract entities. On such an interpretation, the mods would be ontologically akin to sets or numbers, at least on a Platonist conception of sets and numbers. Perhaps it would be less controversial to recognise the mods as infinite were one to view them as abstract. But the existence of abstract objects is a controversy in itself. A good Ockhamist would try to avoid positing abstracta or, if refusing to admit any is not an option, posit as few as possible. I will not here examine the claim that there are abstracta that could fairly be called 'RMT mods'.[1] In this book, I pursue the line of thought that it is a requirement of normal scientific idealisation that one recognise digital infinity in empirical nature. I will examine the sense in which one can ascribe digital infinity to empirical nature without talking about abstract objects.

There are different forms of scientific idealisation. The kind of idealisation in play for recognising digital infinity is sometimes known as minimalist idealisation. Michael Weisberg characterises minimalist idealisation as 'the practice of constructing and studying theoretical models that include only the core causal factors which give rise to a phenomenon... [A] minimalist model contains only those factors that *make a difference* to the occurrence and essential character of the phenomenon in question' (Weisberg, 2007,

---

[1] Although I have elsewhere. See Bolender (2010, Ch. 6).

p. 642; cf. Strevens, 2008, Ch. 8). I would go further: one must sometimes subtract irrelevant features even to recognise an interesting phenomenon in the first place.[2] On a minimalist model for language or social-relational cognition, the constraining influence of performance factors is subtracted. This reveals the interesting phenomenon of indefinite recursion. Since performance factors are never absent, the minimalist idealisation yields a description of a counterfactual.

Postal dismisses the appeal to counterfactuals as unscientific. '[I]f there were infinite time and the human brain were infinite, then a biological production of tokens could have an infinite output. But real inquiry is not concerned with things which could exist if the world were different than it is' (Postal, 2009, p. 112). Contrary to Postal's second sentence, science is concerned with how the world would be if, counterfactually, certain conditions had been different. The nature of scientific laws illustrates this. A scientific law is not simply a true generalisation, but must also support counterfactuals. 'Laws of nature are in fact commonly used to justify subjunctive and contrary-to-fact conditionals, and such use is characteristic of all nomological universals' (Nagel, 1979, p. 51). It is the task of science to map 'the very sinews of causation', to borrow a phrase from Ted Honderich, sinews which he identifies with 'Certain conditional connections in the world' (Honderich, 2004, p. 9). These include counterfactuals.

Robert Batterman uses the chaos game to illustrate how minimalist idealisation is, at least in some cases, crucial for arriving at a good explanation (1992; 2002b, pp. 23f). It also illustrates how the explanandum itself can be counterfactual. The chaos game begins by taking a piece of paper and marking off three vertices of a triangle. Label one vertex (1, 2), label another vertex (3, 4), and label the remaining

[2] Minimalist idealisation has been defended by several philosophers of science (Putnam, 1975; Jackson and Pettit, 1988; Cartwright, 1989; Batterman, 2000; 2002a; 2002b; Weisberg, 2007; Strevens, 2008), at least one physicist (Baxter, 1982), and at least one biologist (Thompson, 1942, pp. 1029f). It is, although not often explicitly stated, evidently widely taken for granted in physics and chemistry.

vertex (5, 6). Suppose that you start at point (1, 2). You roll a regular six-sided die. Suppose it lands on four. That corresponds to point (3, 4). The rule of the game says to make a black point between your starting point (1, 2) and the point indicated by the die (3, 4). This in-between point becomes your new starting point. You then roll the die again, and repeat *ad infinitum*. Literally a*d infinitum*. As you continue, a pattern emerges. The black points you are making correspond to the fractal pattern of what is known as a Sierpiński triangle or Sierpińksi gasket (Figure 2).[3]

Figure 2

Approximation to a Sierpiński triangle. An actual Sierpiński triangle consists of smaller and smaller triangles *ad infinitum*.

As no one lives forever, no one plays the chaos game forever. But the Sierpiński pattern is infinite. This means that no actual performance of the game yields a true Sierpiński triangle. In fact, one could easily conceive of a playing of the game which does not even begin to approximate the pattern. For example, one could conceivably roll 1, 3, 1, 3, 1, 3, 1,

---

[3] There are different forms of the chaos game yielding various fractal patterns (Peitgen *et al.*, 2004, Ch. 6).

Kinds of Idealisation 29

3, 1, 3, 1, 3 and so on. Suppose the 1-3 pattern repeats for 10,000 rolls of the die. All resulting black points would lie on the same line, and nothing bearing the Sierpiński gestalt would be seen. Conceivably, the 1-3 pattern could extend to infinity. In this sense, the chaos game is not guaranteed to yield the Sierpiński pattern. However, the sequence 1, 3, 1, 3, 1, 3, 1, 3, 1, 3, 1, 3 is very improbable, given that one is playing with a fair die. As the sequence continues in the same 1-3 manner, the entire sequence becomes increasingly less probable. In other words, 20,000 consecutive rolls exhibiting the 1-3 pattern is less probable than 10,000 consecutive rolls exhibiting that pattern. Asymptotically, the probability deflates to zero at infinity. Given the laws of large numbers, all playings of the chaos game yield the Sierpiński triangle. One must idealise, in minimalist fashion, in order to recognise that the chaos game always produces a Sierpiński triangle. One idealises by factoring out at least one performance limitation: death. This is a case in which performance limitations must be removed even to recognise an interesting explanandum in the first place.

Given the explanandum, one must also idealise, in the minimalist manner, to arrive at a good explanation of it. Consider the collection of all infinite playings of the chaos game. One could explain the Sierpiński pattern separately for each playing, without idealising by appealing to the microphysics of the fair die and the flat rigid surface upon which it falls. Such knowledge is needed to explain why the die falls as it does with each roll. This non-idealised explanation would be horrendously complex. In fact, it would be infinite, since the number of die rollings would be infinite. How would one explain the appearance of the Sierpiński triangle for the collection of all infinite games? One could do so by conjoining the microphysical explanations for all infinite games into one single grand explanation. Grand but awful. It would be an atrocious explanation. Arguably, it would not be an explanation at all, since it would contain too much irrelevant information to be illuminating.

The best explanation, as Batterman notes, appeals to the laws of large numbers (Batterman, 1992, p. 333). Those laws entail the following: as the number of rolls goes to infinity, the probability of the relative frequency of a fair die landing on one plus the probability of the relative frequency of a fair die landing on two plus the probability of the relative frequency of a fair die landing on three plus the probability of the relative frequency of a fair die landing on four plus the probability of the relative frequency of a fair die landing on five plus the probability of the relative frequency of a fair die landing on six equal 1. It is for this reason that the Sierpiński pattern appears generically in the limit. In fact, the probability of the pattern appearing at the limit is unity. Note that this explanation is highly abstract,[4] factoring out the various sequences of die outcomes for each playing of the chaos game. It also factors out the microphysics upon which each sequence depends. These details are irrelevant, and factoring out irrelevant details is what minimalist idealisation is all about.

Is this a deviant case of explanation? Is it relevantly like uncontroversial cases of scientific explanation? Let us consider some examples showing that it is not deviant. Consider the Ising model in which atoms, or other particles, are represented as points on a lattice or graph. Each point is allowed to be in only one of two states and only to interact with its nearest neighbours. As Weisberg notes, the model is 'extremely simple, building in almost no realistic detail about the substances being modeled' (2007, p. 642). For this reason, as noted by the physicist Rodney Baxter, 'There are "down-to-earth" physicists and chemists who reject lattice models as being unrealistic. In its most extreme form, their argument is that if a model can be solved exactly, then it must be pathological', a view which Baxter dismisses as 'defeatist nonsense' (1982, p. v). He goes on to note that the model predicts properties common to fluids. More specifically, it predicts a mathematical property, the critical exponent, which describes the behaviour of fluid density as a function of temperature near the critical temperature for the

---

[4] It is not abstract in the sense in which numbers and sets are abstract, namely existing outside space and time. It is, rather, abstract in the sense of leaving out many details.

liquid/vapour transition. 'More remarkable still is the fact that the very *same* critical exponent β apparently describes the behavior of magnets as they undergo a transition from the ferromagnetic state with positive net magnetiszation below the critical point, to the paramagnetic phase with zero magnetization above the critical point' (Batterman, 2002a, p. 24). The exponent β is a mathematical property that is only predicted by making unrealistic idealisations. Likewise with the appearance of the full Sierpiński triangle at the limit of the chaos game. Likewise with the digital infinity of language and the digital infinity of mods. Mods and language share a common formal property, but this is only revealed by making what Evans and Levinson call 'a radical distinction between competence and performance' (2009, p. 482).

Once one performs a minimalist idealisation, one finds indefinite recursion in a number of systems: rangeomorphs, fungi, DNA, language, unbounded counting, and social-relational cognition. In other words, indefinite recursion is what philosophers call a multiply realised property (Block and Fodor, 1972; Putnam, 1975). Multiple realisation is the occurrence of the same macro property in systems that are radically different on a micro level. Batterman hypothesises that multiple realisation is the same as what physicists call 'universality' (2000). The critical exponent is multiply realised because it appears in physically distinct systems.

The discovery of a feature shared across a number of microphysically diverse systems is one important reason for performing a minimalist idealisation in the first place. Such a shared feature often enjoys a common explanation which itself requires minimalist idealisation. Far from losing touch with reality, minimalist idealisation reveals facets of reality.

Brownian motion provides another illustration. Brownian motion is the apparently random movement of particles suspended in a fluid. The movement of any given particle is unpredictable, but one can predict the average velocity of all the particles. By noting that particles move faster, on average, as the fluid grows hotter, Einstein argued for the existence of molecules. He reasoned that molecules bombard particles more frequently as the temperature increases. The result is an increase in the average rate of particle velocity. The explanandum here is the increase in average particle velocity. The explanans is the existence of molecules bombarding the much larger particles. But note that the explanandum is already an abstraction. To speak of the average velocity of all the particles is to ignore the trajectories and velocities of each individual particle. One could describe the state of the system of particles and fluid without mentioning average velocity, by giving details for each particle. There is even a sense in which this description would be complete, leaving nothing out. In that sense, it is a concrete explanandum. The abstract explanandum is multiply realised in the sense of appearing in systems consisting of the same particles in the same fluid at the same temperature. But if one focused on the behaviour of each individual particle, one would not find universality. One would find difference. Each system would consist of particles behaving differently. Noticing universality in such systems requires abstraction.

Hilary Putnam offers what has come to be a classic illustration of minimalist idealisation in explanation (1975, pp. 295–96). Putnam asks us to imagine a board with two holes. One hole is a circle one inch in diameter. The other hole is a square one inch across. There is also a peg. The peg is square and one-sixteenth of an inch shy of being one inch on a side. The explanandum is that the peg can pass through the square hole but not the round hole. As Putnam observes, 'The explanation is that the board is rigid, the peg is rigid, and as a matter of geometrical fact, the round hole is smaller than the peg, the square hole is bigger than the cross-section of the peg. The peg passes through the hole that is large enough to take its cross-section, and does not pass through the hole that is too small to take its cross-section' (*ibid.*, p. 296).

Despite the obviousness of Putnam's explanation, calling it the best explanation clashes with some widely held views. According to Michael Taylor, 'A good explanation should

Kinds of Idealisation 33

be, amongst other things, as *fine-grained* as possible', and likewise Jon Elster who remarked that 'a more detailed explanation is also an end in itself' (both quoted in Jackson and Pettit, 1992, p. 1). If Taylor and Elster are right, the best explanation for the square peg failing to pass through the round hole would lie on the level of micro-physics. As Putnam notes, one could describe the peg and board on a microphysical level, a level that would not even mention roundness or squareness *per se*. Such a deduction would be enormously complex. Putnam suggests that this deduction would not be an explanation at all due to its extreme complexity. But, not wanting to quibble over words, he concedes that one could stipulate that it is some kind of explanation. 'If you want to, let us say that the deduction *is* an explanation, it is just a terrible explanation, and why look for terrible explanations when good ones are available?' (Putnam, 1975, p. 296). What makes the simple, common sense explanation the best one is that it leaves out irrelevant details. It is a kind of misrepresentation, since the micro-level events clearly crucially enter into the occurrence of the explanandum. But it is a misrepresentation that improves the explanatory power of the model (Strevens, 2008, p. 300).

The need to abstract in order to isolate important explananda and explanantia is illustrated with a thought experiment discussed by Daniel Dennett, which he attributes to Robert Nozick. Suppose that there are organisms of intelligence vastly greater than our own from some other planet. 'They can be supposed to be Laplacean super-physicists, capable of comprehending the activity on Wall Street, for instance at the microphysical level. Where we see brokers and buildings and sell orders and bids, they see vast congeries of subatomic particles milling about—and they are such good physicists that they can predict days in advance what ink marks appear each day on the paper tape labeled "Closing Dow Jones Industrial Average"' (Dennett, 1987, p. 25). Because they can make predictions based on information from the micro level alone, they do not need to ascribe beliefs and desires to people. Beliefs and desires, after all, don't appear on the atomic level.

Despite their impressive powers, Dennett notes that the space aliens would be blind to perfectly objective patterns in human behaviour. They would be blind to patterns which can only be described in terms of beliefs and desires. Considered on the micro level, there are indefinitely many physical processes which would constitute a certain sort of action, e.g. expressing the desire to dump one's stock in a company. There are indefinitely many different means for contacting one's financial advisor, indefinitely many different ways of wording one's desire. Microphysically, these are different types of processes. But on a macro level, the level corresponding to ascriptions of beliefs and desires, they are all of the same type. Their effect on the stock market, as described on a macro level, would also all be the same.

Postal may have misunderstood the sort of idealisation at issue here. He writes 'The invocation of [idealisation in attributing indefinite recursion to a mental faculty - *jb*] has nothing in common with its sensible use, as when in making certain practical physical calculations one idealises to a system in which there is no friction. The "idealisation" here is rather parallel to one which claims the solar system has an infinity of planets (e.g. of tinier and tinier sizes filling the spaces between the usually cited planets)' (Postal, 2009, p. 110). When Postal speaks of a 'sensible use' of idealisation he appears, in fact, to be talking about what Weisberg calls Galilean idealisation (Weisberg, 2007). In Galilean idealisation, one distorts a theory to make it simpler, and one makes it simpler in order to reduce a computational burden. Subtracting friction from a system is often a means for making calculations more tractable. When one can calculate without the simplifying distortions, then the distortions are dropped. In other words, Galilean idealisation is purely pragmatic. Note Postal's example of idealising to a system without friction and his reference to 'practical physical calculations'. Postal may be assuming that Galilean idealisation is the only legitimate sort of idealisation. If so, then the examples given earlier are a challenge to his view. The earlier idealisations were not merely pragmatic, although in some cases they may have been pragmatic as well. They were acts of disregarding the irrelevant. This is the difference between minimalist idealisation versus Galilean idealisation.

Further, turning to his example of the planets: supposing a non-actual astronomical infinity is not as absurd as Postal imagines. Scientists observe symmetries in nature, including translational symmetries, glide symmetries, and dilational symmetries. But, strictly speaking, nothing empirical exhibits translational symmetry or glide symmetry or dilational symmetry. A thing would have to be infinitely extended to have any of those symmetries (Stewart and Golubitsky, 1992, e.g. p. 264). Scientists speak of a spiral galaxy, for example, as having a combination of rotational and dilational symmetry. This means that if you shrink the galaxy the right amount and rotate it to the appropriate angle, it will look the same as it did beforehand. Of course, the sentence I just typed is literally false. If one could do that to a spiral galaxy, it would not look the same. It would look smaller. The effect could only literally be achieved if the spiral shape extended both outward and inward infinitely. Of course, it doesn't. But scientists idealise by ignoring this, and recognise symmetry in the galaxy anyway. It then becomes a question for astrodynamics how to explain this symmetry. If the minimalist idealisation were not made, the explanandum would not be recognised in the first place. But one would not even recognise the spiral galaxy as having any non-trivial symmetries without performing an idealisation strikingly similar to the one dismissed by Postal. One treats the galaxy as infinite by subtracting constraints on its implementation, in some sense of 'implementation'. Likewise, one treats the mods as infinite by subtracting constraints on their implementation. Then a question arises for the mods, as it did for the spiral galaxy, namely how to explain the mathematical property thus revealed.

Fiske's distinction between mods and preos is also a minimalist idealisation. By considering mods in isolation from preos, the formal properties of mods are revealed. These formal properties turn out to be multiply realised, even commonly found in inorganic systems. Fiske discusses how each basic mod resembles one of the four classic measurement scales (1991, p. 210). Communal Sharing shares formal properties with a nominal scale; Authority Ranking shares formal features with an ordinal scale; and so on. He idealises in making this observation, for it is the mods specifically which have these formal properties. Preos are irrelevant. Fiske's idealisation revealed mods to form a descending chain of symmetry subgroups, a property which is shared by systems throughout nature that undergo symmetry breaking (Bolender, 2007a; 2008; 2010). This would include processes as seemingly unrelated to interpersonal cognition as the formation of a snowflake, hurricane, or spiral galaxy. Comparing the development of a mod + preo combination with such inorganic phenomena as snowflake formation would be absurd. The various attitudes toward time, for example, found in the relational models have no evident correlation in H_2O phase transitions. But mods considered in isolation from preos can be compared to such transitions due to similar formal properties. Abstracting out performance limitations reveals yet another formal property of mods apparently multiply realised across a range of diverse systems, namely indefinite recursion.

When philosophers discuss multiple realisation, it is usually the physical multiple realisation of some mental property or other which concerns them (e.g. Putnam, 1975, p. 436). In discussing how the same psychological state could be realised in radically different microphysical structures, Ned Block and Jerry Fodor have appealed to convergent evolution as a possible factor. 'Psychological similarities across species may often reflect convergent environmental selection rather than underlying physiological similarities. For example, we have no particular reason to suppose that the physiology of pain in man must have much in common with the physiology of pain in phylogenetically remote species' (Block and Fodor, 1972, p. 161). As applied to indefinite recursion, the suggestion may initially

Kinds of Idealisation

seem rather incredible. In what sense are rangeomorphs, language and relational cognition all solutions to the same environmental problem? If they are, then the problem must be a very general one. What could it be?

Hierarchical embedding provides stability in complex structures. The widespread need for a structure to keep from falling apart may explain why so many systems exhibit this property. Herbert Simon used a nice example to illustrate the usefulness of hierarchical embedding. He described two watchmakers, who have two fundamentally different ways of constructing watches.

> The watches the men made consisted of about 1,000 parts each. Tempus had so constructed his that if he had one partially assembled and had to put it down—to answer the phone, say—it immediately fell to pieces and had to be reassembled from the elements. The better the customers liked his watches, the more they phoned him, and the more difficult it became for him to find enough uninterrupted time to finish a watch.
>
> The watches Hora handled were no less complex than those of Tempus. But he had designed them so that he could put together subassemblies of about ten elements each. Ten of these subassemblies, again, could be put together into a larger subassembly; and a system of ten of the latter constituted the whole watch. Hence, when Hora had to put down a partly assembled watch in order to answer the phone, he lost only a small part of his work, and he assembled his watches in only a fraction of the man-hours it took Tempus. (Simon, 1962, p. 470)

The usefulness of hierarchical embedding has been used to predict organic molecular structures. Before Linus Pauling arrived at the precisely correct alpha-helical structure of the polypeptide chain, the physicist H.R. Crane reasoned that biological macromolecules were likely to have some helical shape or other. Donald Casper remarked that 'During the war, Crane had been working on problems of assembly line operation. After the war he recognized that the principle in assembling biological structure was analogous to a subassembly manufacturing process: larger structures could most efficiently be built out of smaller structures. He built simple models out of matchboxes, for example, sticking matchboxes together in the same way, arriving at a helix naturally by using the same pair-wise connections repeatedly' (quoted in Hargittai and Hargittai, 2000, p. 93).

Batterman, by contrast, has tried to explain multiply realised properties in terms of probabilities (2000). Thanks to laws of probability, many micro level differences across systems cancel out, a shared property thus emerging on a macro level. These are not necessarily competing accounts. It could be a matter of probabilities that indefinite recursion emerges in microphysically distinct systems, natural selection taking advantage of such a probabilistic tendency in order to build stable structures. This would be analogous to the transparency of protein crystallins being exapted into a functional role within the eye.

Gould remarked upon how the proteins composing the eye lens earlier had different functions in the body. It was a stroke of luck that these same molecules make good material for lenses (Gould, 2002, pp. 1242, 1259, and 1282; cf. Andley, 2006). The proteins were preadapted for their future role in the lens. Their transparency, speaking more specifically, is a spandrel. The proteins themselves underwent a functional shift. But the *transparency* of the proteins did not undergo such a shift, since the transparency itself had no function before it entered into the function of the eye. The transparency, in a sense, just happened. There may be a sense in which indefinite recursion 'just happens' whilst natural selection takes advantage of the structural stability of this property and puts it to work.[5]

Note that Chomsky does not hold the view that indefinite recursion is widely multiply realised. Rather, he emphasises its rareness. Digital infinity 'is virtually unknown in the biological world. There are plenty of continuous systems, plenty of finite systems but try to find a system of discrete infinity!... there seems to be no analogue elsewhere in the biological world down to the level of,

---

[5] A specific version of this view is defended in Hauser *et al.* (2002), *viz.* that while the computational core of language (presumably Merge) is not an adaptation itself, natural selection has put it to use in cognition and communication. That is, it is a spandrel.

maybe, DNA or some level where you are talking about biochemistry really' (Chomsky, 2000a, p. 52). He is very much aware that the faculty for counting also exhibits indefinite recursion, but views the indefinite recursion of language as being a cause of the indefinite recursion of counting. Counting is an 'abstraction from' (1988, p. 169) or 'offshoot of' (2000a, p. 52) language, as he has put it. The multiple-realisation conception of indefinite recursion, the view on offer here, is an alternative to Chomsky's 'offshoot' view. The indefinite recursion of both counting and language may reflect the multiple realisability of indefinite recursion. If so, then Merge is multiply realised. Fractal branching, for example, is Merge-like in that it produces hierarchical structures potentially without limit.

It is psychological properties which are usually taken to be multiply realised. Occasionally, one hears about a non-psychological property being multiply realised, e.g. Batterman's discussion of criticality. But either way, a multiply realised property is usually taken to be consistently psychological or non- psychological. What is surprising about Merge is that it is psychological in some contexts (such as language) while being non-psychological in others (fungi, rangeomorphs). Although this may sound strange to those familiar with the philosophical literature on multiple realisation, it is implicit in Chomsky's remark that *any* system of digital infinity utilises Merge.[6]

Chomsky's reasoning seems to be that indefinite recursion is biologically so rare that it must be inherently improbable. Assuming improbability, it is plausible to view the indefinite recursion of one system as an offshoot of the indefinite recursion of the other. This would be more plausible than positing two wholly distinct systems of a highly improbable sort. A supporting consideration concerns adaptation, or the lack of it: unbounded counting is clearly

---

[6] I know of no objection to a property existing in both psychological and non-psychological contexts, but *that* sort of multiple realisation is not commonly discussed in the relevant philosophical literature. The term 'multiple realisation' usually appears in discussions of mind–body reduction.

not an adaptation, since it often remains unused by peoples living in conditions similar to the ancestral environment. Language, by contrast, is an adaptation.[7] Therefore, plausibly, language evolved and counting is simply a resourceful extension of language. All of this should be qualified, however, with Chomsky's cautious remarks about evolutionary explanations often being wild guesses. He clearly means to include his own speculations.[8]

But indefinite recursion is not so biologically rare. In addition to the genetic code, one also finds indefinite recursion in rangeomorphs, fungi (Golinski *et al.*, 2008 and references) and bacteria cultures (Fujikawa and Matsushita, 1989; Matsuyama and Matsushita, 1993). This observation begins to undermine Chomsky's argument for indefinite recursion in counting being an offshoot from indefinite recursion in language. Rather, indefinite recursion begins to look like a 'universal' as Baxter (1982) uses the term. It is a mathematical property that emerges in physically distinct systems—just as the mathematical property of forming a descending symmetry subgroup chain emerges in physically distinct systems due to spontaneous symmetry breaking.

There is independent evidence that unbounded counting is not an offshoot of syntax. Varley *et al.* (2005) have shown that linguistic recursive deficit can be accompanied by arithmetical competence. Although it may surprise some, Varley and her colleagues do not believe that the outcome refutes Chomsky: '[L]anguage grammar might provide a "bootstrapping" template to facilitate the use of other hierarchical and generative systems, such as mathematics.

---

[7] To speak more carefully, the faculty of language *in the broad sense* (Hauser *et al.*, 2002) is an adaptation.

[8] It is just as plausible, I submit, to view counting as an exaptation from the system of mods. Digital infinity is not the only property relevant to judging whether counting might be exapted from the mod-building system. The elementary mods correspond to basic arithmetical operations (Fiske, 1991, pp. 210–20). This raises the possibility that the integer system is the system of mods without the preonic systems. Three elements of the human number sense can be distinguished: the analogue system, the 1-2-3 system, and digital infinity. The latter two can be found in the mod-building system.

However, once those resources are in place, mathematics can be sustained without the grammatical and lexical resources of the language faculty' (*ibid.*, p. 3523). But a different result would have corroborated Chomsky, while the actual result did not. Hence, the result is soft evidence that counting and grammar are causally independent. I submit that viewing indefinite recursion as multiply realised is at least an alternative to Chomsky's view that it is unique to language. This somewhat weakens Chomsky's argument that counting is an offshoot of the computatinal core of language.

Summary

Recognising digital infinity, whether in relational cognition or in language, requires distinguishing competence from performance. The distinction is a kind of idealisation, specifically a minimalist idealisation in which certain details are left out due to their irrelevance. Some criticism of the competence/performance distinction results from a failure to appreciate the importance of minimalist idealisation in science, falsely assuming that all legitimate idealisation is Galilean. Minimalist idealisation often reveals a property to be multiply realised, digital infinity being a case in point. Once constraints on implementation are factored out, one finds digital infinity to be widely realised, contrary to the view that it is biologically rare or perhaps even unique to language. Numerous instances of indefinite recursion in biology also weaken Chomsky's case.

Chapter Three

Building the Infinite

We have noted that the systematicity and broad variety of social structures suggests a combinatorial operation. The digital infinity of the mods suggests Merge in particular. Being set-constructive, a Merge-based grammar is set-theoretic. Set-theoretical grammars are a subclass of proof-theoretical grammars. The linguists Terence Langendoen and Paul Postal[1] characterise proof-theoretic grammars for natural languages as follows: 'Given some non-finite collection, one can demand a finite characterisation. One such type is a finitistic, proof-theoretic or constructive system, a Turing machine... Such devices consist of a finite set of operations with a fixed mode of application such that after a finite number of steps any element of the set to be characterised is specified' (1984, p. 17, emphasis deleted). The mental faculty yielding complex mods fits this characterisation of a Turing machine insofar as a mod is embedded within another mod which can, in turn, be embedded in yet another mod — i.e. a step-by-step procedure — until the process halts with the production of a completed complex mod.

Some speculation about how the brain does this is already implicit in Fiske, who speaks of two operations, which he identifies as 'recursion' and 'composition' (1991, pp. 150f) . He also sometimes speaks of 'concatenation' and 'embedding' as the two operations. Fiske and his colleagues have also written of 'concatenations and nested hierarchies'

---

[1] So as to avoid possible confusion, note that Langendoen and Postal describe proof-theoretic grammars for natural languages as a step toward dismissing them. This matter will be discussed later.

Building the Infinite 43

in social structures (Fiske *et al.*, 1991, p. 658). The term 'nested' in linguistics is usually reserved for centre-embedded constructions, such as *The philosopher, who was quite fat, broke the chair*, the sub-clause being underlined. The more general term 'embedded' includes right-recursion as well as centre-embedding. *The parson fell through a crack, because he was so thin* illustrates right-recursion. It is not clear how, or if at all, the distinction between nesting and right-recursion translates into complex social structures. I suggest avoiding the word 'nesting' in social-relational cognition in favour of the more generic 'embedding'.

What operations are needed in a grammar for relational cognition? We have already discussed Merge. Might one also need a Copy operation?

In some sense, Copy must be present, but is it a basic operation or is it a special case of Merge? For example, $\{\alpha, \{\alpha\}\}$ can be construed as the result of applying Merge twice, once to α yielding $\{\alpha\}$ and once again both to α and to $\{\alpha\}$ yielding $\{\alpha, \{\alpha\}\}$. This would be equivalent to copying α into a higher position in the structure but without using a distinct Copy operation (cf. Chomsky, 2003, p. 307; Boeckx, 2008, p. 29). There would be no Copy, because it is numerically the same α in both positions. That is, the same token occurs in both positions.

For some reflection on the type/token distinction, consider the following passage from Boruch Brody: '[A token is a] specified utterance of a linguistic expression or a written occurrence of it. An expression-*type*, on the other hand, is an entity abstracted from all actual and potential occurrences of a linguistic expression. In "John loves John," for example, there are three word-tokens but only two word-types' (Brody, 1967, p. 76). The type/token distinction, for this discussion, is applied to mental symbols. A single mental-symbol type can be multiply tokened in the brain-mind. The Copy operation, if there is one, produces multiple tokens of a given type. The type/token distinction can also be applied to operations.

Note that when I speak of Merge in language and Merge in social-relational cognition, I am not necessarily speaking of numerically the same operation. In other words, these could be two tokens of the same type of operation. This would be so if indefinite recursion is multiply realised in different types of neural structure. Hypothetically, one token Merge could break down while the other token Merge remains intact. If Merge is multiply realisable, as suggested here, then there could be three distinct Merge operations for language, relational cognition and counting respectively.

It may still be necessary to posit Copy, as a basic operation, for the social-relational computational system for a different reason. If all of the elementary mods result from a single mental faculty, a 'Social Pattern Generator' (SPG), which can only represent one mod at a time, then Copy is essential. Nothing compound can occur within the SPG. A representation of a mod has to be copied from the SPG so that its copies can enter into compound mods. A case for an SPG producing all four basic mods through spontaneous symmetry breakings is made in Bolender (2010).[2]

The following is a possible grammar for relational cognition. It is chosen for its extreme simplicity, raising a methodological question: is the simplest grammar also the most plausible? I submit that one should begin with that, and only complicate it as new evidence forces one to do so.

The proposed grammar consists of five *primes*, two *operations*, three *syntactic rules* and two *semantic rules*.

---

[2] Aoun *et al.* raise a similar consideration arguing for Copy in language:
'[T]here is a (virtually unanimously held) distinction between the lexicon and the computational system and that words are accessed from the lexicon. How does Copy follow from this fact? It is universally assumed ... the atoms manipulated by the computational system come from the lexicon. How does the computational system access the lexicon? It does so by copying elements from the lexicon to the computational system. That accessing the lexicon involves copying is clear from the fact that the lexicon gets no smaller when it is accessed and words are obtained for manipulation by the syntax. If this is correct, then grammars that distinguish the lexicon from the computational system conceptually presuppose an operation like Copy. As virtually every approach to grammar assumes something like a distinction between lexicon and grammar, Copy is a "virtually conceptually necessary" operation...' (Aoun *et al.*, 2001, p. 400)

Primes

c = CS, a = AR, e = EM, m = MP, n = Null[3]

Operations

Copy: copies items from the lexicon

Merge: constructs sets from objects already constructed

Syntactic rules

1. Every derivation has a last step.

   This is necessary for the set of all mods to be Turing computable.

2. At most one prime is merged at a time.

3. At least one prime is merged at a time. Hence, an expression of the form $\{\{\alpha\}\}$ is ill formed.

   The combination of 2 and 3 guarantees that any mod will belong to exactly one relational type.

Semantic rules

4. Only a set can be interpreted as a social relatum.

5. A dominant prime determines the type of relation.

To illustrate both semantic rules, {a, {m}} would not be interpreted as a relation between a group structured by AR and another group structured by MP. Rather, it would indicate an MP relation embedded in an AR relation. Further, in {a, {m}}, 'a' is the dominant prime. {c, {e, {m}}} would be a CS relation dominating an EM relation which dominates an MP relation.

Examples

{c, {c, {c, {c, {c, {c}}}}}}; i.e. a CS level embedded in a CS level embedded in a CS level, and so on. The earlier discussion of the <u>buudu</u> among the Moose would be an example. The

---

[3] I omit discussion of the hypothetical elementary model Oceanic Merging, since it does not appear to enter into compound mods. For discussion, see Bolender (2010).

expression results from six applications of Merge. The expression does not capture how many social relata are to be found on each level. It does not reflect the number of families represented on the most subordinate level, for example. This would be a matter for preonic interpretation. This is as it should be, since one can mentally represent such a layered society without necessarily thinking about the individual units on a given layer. Thinking about individual units is evidently an additional mental ability.

{a, {m}}; i.e. an AR relation with an MP component. One example would be the relation between judge and defendant. Fundamentally, the relation is AR. But the judge employs MP in deciding on a punishment proportional to the crime, if any.

{m, {a}}; i.e. an MP relation with an AR component. An example would be the relation between customer and waiter in a restaurant. There is clearly an authority relation, but the fundamental relation is one of payment for services rendered.

{a, {m}, {n}}; i.e. an AR relation between at least one group structured by MP and at least one other group falling under the Null model. Preonic systems would determine which groups are the authority and which subordinate. An example would be Nietzche's conception of the relation between masters and slaves in antiquity from the masters' viewpoint. For Nietzsche, relations between masters were structured by MP. 'Every thing has its price: *everything* can be compensated for… Justice… is the good will, between those who are roughly equal, to come to terms with each other, to "come to an understanding" again by means of settlement' (Nietzsche, 1994, p. 50). This is represented here as '{m}'. The slaves, at least initially, are seen by the masters as being structured by no model at all, i.e. the Null relation: 'The good men are a caste; the bad men are a multitude, like particles of dust' (Nietzsche, 1984, p. 47). This is represented here as '{n}'. The authority of masters over slaves is represented as 'a' in the dominant position; hence '{a, {m}, {n}}'.

There is some ambiguity in the grammar. {X, {Y}} could either represent a Y-group embedded in an X-group or a relation structured by both X and Y but with Y subordinated to X. Preonic systems could interpret such an expression either way.

There is a one-one mapping between mods and expressions generated by the above grammar. Or, at least, that is the goal. The grammar reveals the precise relations between complex mods. In doing so, we see that it is not necessary to introduce two distinct combinatorial operations, as Fiske sometimes does. Both recursion and composition are special cases of embedding, given the simplest possible grammar. For example, {a, {a}} and {m, {a}} are both instances of embedding. Another benefit of formulating such a grammar is that it makes possible an intuitive grasp of mods as interrelated structures. The nature and interrelations of the complex mods just make sense when seen in terms of the grammar proposed (cf. Black, 1962).

The grammar, however, includes no account of the system's capacity to produce the primes. In the case of the four elementary mods, these plausibly result from self-organisation (Bolender, 2010). The full account, then, is both dynamicist and computational, contrary to tendencies to see these two approaches as hostile to one another (e.g. van Gelder, 1995; van Gelder and Port, 1995).

As discussed earlier, there is already empirical corroboration for the role of the elementary relational models in informing relational cognition. But what of corroboration for the claim that complex mods play a role? A first step in acquiring such corroboration is to have a means of specifying just what the complex mods are. Note that psychological experiments testing RMT began with a typology of the basic mods. In order to further test RMT, one also needs a typology of the complex mods. The grammar proposed above provides just that. Further, given that there must be performance limitations on the generation of complex mods, the ability to specify each mod gives us the means to ask precisely where such limitations enter in. Vague talk of recursion and composition does not do this. The ability to specify each mod also brings in reductive potential. One cannot ask how complex relational cognition is reducible to neuroscience until one has the means to specify each mod. On a classical model of intertheoretic reduction (Nagel, 1979; Churchland, 1986), each property in the science to be reduced requires a nomically coextensive property in the reducing science. One cannot inquire into the evidence for reducibility until one has a specification of the properties of the science to be reduced. The grammar presented here provides that specification (cf. Putnam, 1997). This does not constitute empirical corroboration, but it does show us how to begin to look for such corroboration, as a neuroscientific reduction for a computational theory of relational cognition would clearly count as empirical evidence for the latter.

To say that there are syntactic rules is not to say that such rules are encoded in the system. Maybe they are; maybe they are not. It is perfectly possible that interfacing interpretive systems simply cannot read a structure such as {a, c}. One finds this same sort of thing in the genetic code. The simplest building blocks of DNA are the nucleotides, four in number: adenine (A), guanine (G), thymine (T), and cytosine (C), arranged along the length of the DNA. DNA is transcribed into RNA which is, in turn, translated into proteins.[4] The semantics of a series of nucleotides is translated into amino acids which are assembled into proteins. A codon is a triplet of nucleotides. Most codons code for amino acids, but some only serve to initiate and terminate the translation from the RNA. ATG is the start codon, represented as AUG in RNA. Three other codons are stop codons. A ribosome, which serves as a translation machine, won't even read a sequence unless it begins with AUG. This is a case in which the distinction between a 'grammatical' versus an 'ungrammatical' expression is not wholly determined by the productive process which creates the genome.

---

[4] For details, see Pierce (2008).

Ribosomes also play a role in sorting well-formed sequences from those that are not well formed. According to Chomsky, there is something at least broadly similar in language, what is known as 'feature checking' (1995). Some logically possible expressions simply cannot be read at the performance interfaces, and thus prove to be invisible to the system. We should be open to the possibility that the syntactic rules in the relational grammar proposed above are not encoded anywhere but reflect limits on the literacy of interfacing systems.

Summary

Given the finite resources of the brain, the digital infinity of relational cognition requires a grammar with a combinatorial procedure, namely a proof-theoretic grammar. Formalisation of this grammar specifies all possible mods and reveals their interrelations. This is a necessary step in reducing RMT to a neuroscientific theory. One must know specifically what cognitive states are in question before addressing the issue of identifying them with states of the brain.

Chapter Four
Universal Moral Grammar

Legend has it that Ernest Rutherford once remarked that 'All science is either physics or stamp collecting.' The observation, whoever first said it, is no doubt unfair, but it highlights something important: there is a difference between explaining versus merely describing. The difference corresponds to two different interpretations of the term 'linguistic universal' or 'universal principle'. Paul Smolensky and Emmanuel Dupoux note an ambiguity in how a reader could interpret these terms, remarking that 'In a theory of cognition, a universal principle is a property true of all human minds—a cog-universal—not a superficial descriptive property true of the expressions of all languages—a des-universal. This is why generative grammar, with its explicit goal of seeking cog-universals, has always been more central to cognitive science than linguistic typology, which only speaks to des-universals' (Smolensky and Dupoux, 2009, p. 468). A descriptive universal is a category applying to all expressions of all natural languages. A cognitive universal, by contrast, is an explanation as to why languages are the way they are. Clearly, Merge and Copy are cognitive universals, if they exist at all. Smolensky and Dupoux believe that many critics of Universal Grammar focus on descriptive universals whilst seeming not to realise that cognitive universals are at issue.

Analogous points apply to relational cognition, including moral cognition. There has been discussion recently of a possible Universal Moral Grammar (UMG) (Harman, 2000,

Ch. 13; Bolender, 2001; Hauser, 2006; Mikhail, 2007). Should one expect UMG to consist of moral principles or to consist of mental operations for constructing them? The former would be a descriptive UMG, the latter a cognitive one. Given that the goal is explanatory depth, the answer should be obvious: as cognitive scientists we mean to investigate the cognitive underpinnings of moral judgment. In the UMG literature, however, the distinction between cognitive versus descriptive universals is not always explicit. For example, in discussing 'initial evidence for UMG', Mikhail notes that 'prohibitions of murder, rape and other types of aggression appear to be universal or nearly so' (2007, p. 143) without clarifying whether these prohibitions are part of UMG or result from it. The phrase 'initial evidence for UMG' could be taken either way. The prohibitions themselves, if universal, are descriptive universals. One digs deeper to find cognitive universals.

What are the cognitive universals of moral judgment from an RMT perspective? What are the links between moral principles and relational models? Fiske has discussed how various moral principles correspond to each elementary model (1991, Ch. 6; Fiske and Ehrenhalt, n.d.). CS informs an ethic of service to the community, to one's group. '[E]veryone acknowledges some ethical duty to care and compassion for others' (Fiske and Ehrenhalt, n.d., p. 10). The CS ethic is an ethic of 'altruism' in some sense, although the identification with others in the group is so strong, one thinks of them as sharing a common identity with oneself. So there is also a sense in which CS is not altruistic. The ethic of AR is reflected in a saying of Mo Tzu: 'Upon hearing good or evil, one shall report it to one's superior. What the superior thinks to be right, all shall think to be right. What the superior thinks to be wrong, all shall think to be wrong' (quoted in Fiske, 1991, p. 117). AR also includes pastoral duties of superiors to their inferiors along with perquisites and privileges assigned to the former. Righteousness is often defined as doing God's will. Failing to respect seniority and age often seems immoral in AR. Ethical principles of equal treatment and compensation, uniform contributions and even distribution are structured by EM. 'The morality of Market Pricing is represented in the libertarian ideology of absolute freedom of rational choice, together with the sanctity of voluntarily negotiated contracts or promises...' (*ibid.*, p. 118).

Merge and Copy must also enter into the construction of moral principles. In the Decalogue, for example, one finds the rule 'Honor your father and your mother, so that your days may be long in the land that the Lord your God is giving you.' The rule illustrates AR, but the motivation to obey the rule also stems from the authority of 'the Lord your God'. Both authorities are part of a single moral principle in which one instance of AR is embedded in a superordinate instance of AR. The traditional Indian practice of Satī, in which a recently widowed woman was burnt alive on her husband's funeral pyre, is evidently a combination of AR and CS. Although the psychological details may have differed from case to case, it was probably often CS subordinated to AR, since the widow was often ordered to perform it. Merge and Copy applied to the mods, further interacting with preos, result in complex moral principles.

From an RMT perspective, UMG is the grammar for relational cognition outlined in the preceding chapter conjoined with preonic interfaces. Although not specialised for moral judgment, the grammar extends to it. These cognitive universals, taken alone, do not predict any descriptive universals. I say 'taken alone', because they could be further constrained, although that would require evidence. The elementary mods, plus what is known about preos, plus Merge and Copy yield a system in which there would be no universal moral principles *unless the system is further complicated in some manner*. What is revealed *so far* are cognitive universals but not a universal moral code (descriptive universals).

The UMG revealed so far implies what Isaiah Berlin called 'pluralism'. Berlin contrasted pluralism with relativism, the latter being the view that cultures differ in their values by virtue of non-rational forces which control and shape one's moral mind. Karl Marx's view that moral values ultimately result from the forces of production would be one sort of relativism. Because people are under the control of these shaping influences, one simply cannot understand or recognise any force in the values of societies that contrast with one's own. Those values are outside the normative domain of one's own society, and hence hardly seem to one like values at all. Pluralism, as Berlin uses the term, is the contrasting view that, while there are fundamentally different systems of value, one can nonetheless come to understand how someone could hold what initially seem like alien values. It is an emotional understanding, not simply the recognition of different causal forces. '"I prefer coffee, you prefer champagne. We have different tastes. There is no more to be said." That is relativism.' Pluralism, by contrast, is 'the conception that there are many different ends that men may seek and still be fully rational, fully men, capable of understanding each other and sympathising and deriving light from each other, as we derive it from reading Plato or the novels of medieval Japan—worlds, outlooks, very different from our own' (Berlin, 1990, p. 11).

Consider Satī again. According to the pluralist, someone in, say, twenty-first-century Paris could relate emotionally to the view that a widow is morally required to perform Satī, even if the Parisian simultaneously condemns the practice. For the relativist, by contrast, the modern Parisian could only understand this practice as a scientist might understand the behaviour of bacteria in a culture medium under a microscope. The gulf between cultures would make emotional identification impossible, on the relativist view. RMT lends some support to the pluralist view. Widow immolation is, after all, a combination of CS and AR, and we all have CS and AR within ourselves.

The ultimate source of variety in moral outlook, the computational system, is shared. That is, we share the means for producing infinitely many moral values drawn from a finite basis. Ironically, though, Berlin believed that pluralism places a finite cap on the number of potential human values.

> I do believe that there is a plurality of values which men can and do seek, and that these values differ. There is not an infinity of them: the number of human values, of values

which I can pursue while maintaining my human semblance, my human character, is finite — let us say 74, or perhaps 122, or 27, but finite, whatever it may be. And the difference this makes is that if a man pursues one of these values, I, who do not, am able to understand why he pursues it or what it would be like, in his circumstances, for me to be induced to pursue it. Hence the possibility of human understanding. (Berlin, 1998, p. 11)[1]

One value in devising a grammar for relational cognition is that the model shows the error in Berlin's reasoning. The grammar shows us how relational cognition, like language, can be what Wilhelm von Humboldt called an 'infinite use of finite media' (quoted in Abler, 1989, p. 1). We share the same finite resources, but, since these resources include a set-constructing operation, human values are potentially infinite.

As noted earlier, there is recursive embedding in the relational cognition of dolphins and baboons, suggesting that this particular infinite use of finite media is not an offshoot of language. More likely, it illustrates the multiple realisation of Merge in different neural systems. Another way to make the same point would be to say that relational cognition utilises a Merge-like procedure that is numerically distinct from Merge in language.

There are, however, some uses of recursion in moral cognition which strongly suggest a role for language. Note that *it is wrong to encourage someone to do something wrong* 'is recursive in the sense that it implies that it is wrong to encourage someone to encourage someone to do something that is wrong, etc. Similarly, a generative moral grammar might imply that it is wrong to promise to do something that it would be wrong to do' (Roedder and Harman, 2010, p. 279). It is hard to see how one could recognise such recursively structured obligations without formulating sentences that express them. The full generative potential of

---

[1] Berlin was also not entirely clear about the distinction between cognitive universals versus descriptive universals as seen in his remark 'all human beings must have some common values or they cease to be human, and also some different values else they cease to differ, as in fact they do' (1998, p. 11). As noted earlier, UMG is not a code of values but the system for constructing such codes.

moral cognition, it would seem, consists of a Merge-like procedure outside language, one shared with baboons and dolphins in their relational cognition, in addition to the combinatorial resources of natural language.

This observation perhaps does some justice to the infinity of morality as discussed by David Hume:

> It may now be ask'd in general, concerning this pain or pleasure, that distinguishes moral good and evil, From what principles is it derived, and whence does it arise in the human mind? To this I reply, first, that 'tis absurd to imagine, that in every particular instance, these sentiments are produc'd by an original quality and primary constitution. For as the number of our duties is, in a manner, infinite, 'tis impossible that our original instincts should extend to each of them, and from our very first infancy impress on the human mind all that multitude of precepts, which are contain'd in the compleatest system of ethics. Such a method of proceeding is not conformable to the usual maxims, by which nature is conducted, where a few principles produce all that variety we observe in the universe, and every thing is carry'd on in the easiest and most simple manner. 'Tis necessary, therefore, to abridge these primary impulses, and find some more general principles, upon which all our notions of morals are founded. (Hume, quoted in Chomsky, 2004, n. 14)

Summary

Universal Moral Grammar (UMG), in the sense of the term that is of interest to cognitive scientists, consists of properties true of all non-pathological human minds. Rather than being itself a moral code, UMG consists of the cognitive mechanisms that most directly enter into the production of moral codes. Different basic relational mods are linked preonically to different moral expectations, evidently due to some neurological necessity. The combination of basic models into compound models, as per the grammar presented in Chapter Three, illustrates how cognitive processes produce complex moral expectations. Being recursive, the grammar also illustrates the potential infinitude of such expectations. The grammar described in Chapter Three, plus the relevant preonic systems with which it interfaces, constitute the cognitive UMG. Its existence supports moral pluralism, as defined by Berlin. Pluralism is the view that, while there are different moral codes, there is also a universally shared capacity to empathetically understand moral codes other than one's own. This understanding serves as the basis for meaningful dialogue on moral issues across cultures.

Chapter Five
Computer Wars

Positing computer models for mental processes is both classic cognitive science and extremely controversial. This chapter reviews some of the controversy insofar as it may pertain to a computer model of RMT.

Consider Langendoen and Postal's characterisation of proof-theoretic grammars yet again: 'a finite set of operations with a fixed mode of application such that after a finite number of steps any element of the set to be characterised is specified' (1984, p. 17). In such a system, one finds a sequence of symbol manipulations consisting of discrete steps, such as would be illustrated in any Chomskyan syntax textbook (e.g. Radford, 1997; Carnie, 2007). The same applies to relational cognition: each embedding is a discrete step in the derivation of a complex mod. Timothy van Gelder and Robert Port, in defending an appeal to dynamics rather than digital computation, note that 'the Turing machine model is inherently incapable of telling us anything at all about the *timing* of these states and the transitions from one state to another. The model just tells us "first this state, then that state..."; it takes no stand on how long the person will be in the first state, how fast the transition to the second state is, and so forth' (van Gelder and Port, 1995, p. 20). This is not the conception of time that one finds in the science of dynamics, as van Gelder and Port are quick to indicate. The time posited in a generative approach 'is not real time, it is mere order' (*ibid.*, p. 20), their point being that a generative approach to cognition is unscientific.

But van Gelder and Port's criticism also fails to take minimalist idealisation into account. The skeletal conception of time, which they dismiss as unscientific, is actually an idealisation. One justification for the idealisation is that it reveals formal similarities across various domains, namely relational cognition, language, rangeomorphs, and suchlike. All exhibit digital infinity and hence require a Merge-like process. Noting differences in temporal properties would be irrelevant and distract from the common explanation.

van Gelder (1995) makes a different sort of mistake. There he shows that it is possible to misconstrue a dynamic system as though it were a digital computer, his illustration being the Watt centrifugal governor. But the governor exhibits continuous infinity, not digital infinity. Hence, it is not the sort of system that would suggest digital computation in the first place.[1] Of course, perhaps some mental faculties are best modelled using the Watt governor, but these, if there are any, would be faculties of mind not exhibiting digital infinity.

Adopting a proof-theoretical approach to relational cognition is not to reject a dynamicist approach to relational cognition. In fact, I have defended a dynamicist approach elsewhere (Bolender, 2007a; 2008; 2010), but that was a dynamicist approach to the *fundamental* models. That degree of dynamicism still leaves open the possibility of a generativist approach to *complex* models. In other words, a dynamicist approach to the basic models leaves open the possibility of the copying of those models and a combinatorial approach to the embedding of those copies.

Let us turn to John Searle's criticism of the view that there are unconscious mental computations. Searle defines cognitivism as the view that cognition consists of algorithmic transformations of symbols (1992). He simplifies this definition by saying that cognitivism is the view that the brain is a digital computer. Cognitive scientists are not nec-

---

[1] Searle makes a similar mistake in his discussion of the vestibular ocular reflex (VOR). Searle notes that the VOR 'has a potentially infinite generative capacity' (1992, p. 235). But this is continuous infinity, not digital infinity. Searle is setting up a straw man when he describes this as the sort of capacity that one might be tempted to explain by appeal to digital computation.

essarily cognitivists according to this definition, although surely some of them are. But it is a classic view within cognitive science that certain specialised mental organs are computational. One version of that view is defended in this book, namely that the mods of compound relational cognition result from a computational operation. Searle's attack on cognitivism in the broader sense is clearly also relevant to the narrower sort of cognitivism at issue here, viz. that a neurocomputational process subserves complex mod building. Any point Searle makes against the broader cognitivism would correspond to a point that he would certainly also direct against a more narrow cognitivism.

Computation is an algorithmic process which respects semantic relations, although being wholly driven by formal properties (Fodor, 1988). It is a syntactic engine imitating a semantic engine, in one classic formulation (Dennett, 1987). For Searle, algorithmic processes which are not even potentially conscious ('deeply unconscious') are conceptually impossible (1992). Therefore, approaches to the mind appealing to such processes are incoherent.

Searle acknowledges that any brain process can be described *as though* it were following an algorithm, but insists that such a description does not correspond to any objective, intrinsic feature of the process. It is executing an algorithm in a mere *as-if* sense. Since science is about discovering objective features, ascribing unconscious computer algorithms to the brain is not science. On Searle's view, no deeply unconscious process is ever intrinsically algorithmic but only algorithmic, if at all, relative to an observer.

Consider a beautiful painting. The painting has some intrinsic properties. It is composed of atoms and has a certain mass; these are properties not requiring an observer. But the painting is only beautiful if someone perceives it as beautiful.[2] Scientific explanations appeal exclusively to intrinsic features. According to Searle, brains are not com-

---

[2] Beauty here is a feature of an object which, when recognised, normally produces a certain sort of subjective emotional response in a sensitive observer. I am not using 'beauty' to mean symmetry, as physicists often do.

puters in any scientifically interesting sense because computation is not intrinsic.

Searle notes that virtually any process can be described *as if* it is a series of digital steps—even if it is a continuous process. He must also be assuming that this is all it means to be digital. Otherwise, he would not say that a neural circuit can only be a digital computer in whatever weak sense that 'stomach, liver, heart, solar system, and the state of Kansas are all digital computers' (1992, p. 208). Frankly, this is not a terribly plausible argument against digital computation being intrinsic. There is a confusion here which, ironically, can perhaps be traced back to Alan Turing himself who noted that 'Everything really moves continuously. But there are many kinds of machines which can profitably be thought of as being discrete state machines. For instance in considering the switches of a lighting system it is a convenient fiction that each switch must be definitely on or definitely off. There must be intermediate positions, but for most purposes we can forget about them' (Turing, 1950, p. 439). It is an idealisation to say that each switch is always definitely on or definitely off. But it is an idealisation made profitable by something perfectly objective, namely the fact that each switch spends the great bulk of its time being either definitely on or definitely off. Only for a fleeting instant is a normally functioning switch in an intermediate position. It is this objective basis for the idealisation that Searle overlooks.

The fact that one can pretend that a continuous process is digital by slicing it up arbitrarily does not imply that this is *all it means* for something to be digital. Granted, the digital shades off into the continuous so that there is no sharp dichotomy between the two. For example, the objective basis for the idealisation could gradually wane, with no clear cut-off point between that which is best described as digital and that which is not. But the absence of a sharp dichotomy does not mean that there is no distinction. A clearly digital phenomenon, such as the spiking of a neuron, is digital. To take a more familiar example, the firefly is clearly doing something that is best counted using natural numbers. These are not matters of subjective interpretation.

But, even if one grants the assumption that being digital is just a matter of interpretation, Searle's argument can still be faulted. To see the point, let's first consider what it is for a process to be algorithmic. Dictionary definitions have it that an algorithm is a procedure, consisting of a finite number of steps, which guarantees or probabilifies a certain result or end-state. So in order for a process to be algorithmic, its behaviour must at the very least be in agreement with such a procedure. That is, it must be describable as though it were following the algorithm. Is this a sufficient condition? It would be extremely permissive to say so. In order for a process to be so describable, it is enough merely that it be describable as following a series of steps ending in a highly probabilified state. Further, all that is required for something to be describable as following a series of steps, given the large assumption we have just granted to Searle, is for it to be decomposable into simpler sequential processes; and all it takes to guarantee or probabilify a certain end-state is for there to be laws of nature.

To grant Searle as much ground as possible, let us assume that being digital is just a matter of arbitrarily slicing up a continuous process, even though this is clearly false for many cases. Making that false assumption, then virtually any process can be interpreted as agreeing with some algorithm or other. For Searle, this shows algorithms to be too cheap to be of any scientific value. Dennett thinks that Searle worries too much.

> [A]re there any limits at all on what may be considered an algorithmic process? I guess the answer is No; if you wanted to, you could treat any process at the abstract level as an algorithmic process. So what? Only some processes yield interesting results when you do treat them as algorithms, but we don't have to try to define 'algorithm' in such a way as to include only the *interesting* ones... The problem will take care of itself, since nobody will waste time examining the algorithms that aren't interesting for one reason or another. It all depends on what needs explaining. (Dennett, 1995, p. 59)

For example, you want to understand how the mind unconsciously parses a sentence. Is the mind using rewrite rules or a combinatorial procedure? Not just any algorithm in the brain is relevant to answering this question. So there is no excessive liberality here to worry about. Everything may be algorithmic, but not every algorithm is an answer to an important question. Or such is Dennett's point.

One worries though that perhaps Dennett is not saying enough. One wants to understand what distinguishes interesting algorithms from trivial ones, rather than just being told that scientists can figure it out for themselves. Intuitively, the trivial algorithms are random, mere flukes; whilst the interesting ones are not. But what does that mean? The answer may vary from one field of science to another. However, for cognitive scientists looking for some implementation of computational processes in neural wetware, the relevant science is biology.

What does the distinction between random and non-random mean for the biologist? Plausibly, it means the distinction between having a function versus not having one. Merge serves as an example. Merge, whether in language or in mod building, is a computational procedure. But it is not such simply because it acts upon lexical items which have semantic contents. It is computational because its *function* is to map signal onto semantics, in the case of language. It is also computational because it has the *function* of producing compositional meanings, both in language and in relational cognition. Having a certain function is a crucial part of what it is for a process to be algorithmic, from a biological perspective.[3] Lexical items can enter into many different causal processes. Function is a means for distinguishing those that are algorithmic from those that are not. This agrees with some dictionary definitions of 'algorithm', according to which an algorithm is a step-by-step procedure 'for accomplishing some end'. The heart intrinsically follows a blood-pumping algorithm partly because its behaviour

---

[3] There is some flexibility of formulation here. One can either say that function is crucial to being algorithmic or that function is crucial to being an algorithm of biological interest.

agrees with such an algorithm but also because it is a function of the heart to produce the end-state of the algorithm, namely the circulation of blood. Furthermore, it is the function of the heart to satisfy that end-state by means of behaving in agreement with the algorithm. By contrast, the heart does not intrinsically follow a make-thumping-sounds algorithm because, even though its behaviour agrees with such an algorithm, it is no function of the heart to make noise.

The cognitivist can say that any deep unconscious brain process intrinsically follows an algorithm if one of its functions is to realise the end-state of that algorithm, and its behaviour agrees with the algorithm for the sake of performing that function. The process is following an algorithm for manipulating symbols on two conditions: the process has semantic properties, and a function of the process is to transform those properties in the relevant manner. This allows for intrinsic algorithmicity without succumbing to the view that all processes are algorithmic.

But Searle tries to block this move by claiming that even functions are observer-relative. He writes that,

> ...when we say that the heart functions to pump blood, the only facts in question are that the heart does, in fact, pump blood; that fact is important to us, and is causally related to a whole lot of other facts that are also important to us, such as the fact that the pumping of blood is necessary to staying alive. If the only thing that interested us about the heart was that it made a thumping noise or that it exerted gravitational attraction on the moon, we would have a completely different conception of its 'functioning' and, correspondingly, of heart disease. To put the point bluntly, in addition to its various causal relations, the heart does not have any functions. When we speak of its functions, we are talking about those of its causal relations to which we attach some *normative* importance. (Searle, 1992, p. 238)

Searle assumes a sturdy fact/value distinction in the spirit of Hume. On such an assumption, the mind superimposes value upon the world by reason of its desires rather than actually discovering value in the world. Values are interpretations rather than facts, that is. If functions presuppose values, then functions are also observer-relative rather than intrinsic. Although the fact/value dichotomy has been challenged (Putnam, 2002), I will assume a sharp distinction throughout in order to grant Searle as much ground as possible. Obviously, if the distinction turns out not to be sharp, this won't help Searle.

There are many purely descriptive analyses of functions (Hempel, 1965; Wright, 1973; Cummins, 1975; Nagel, 1977; Bigelow and Pargetter, 1987), Searle's normative analysis being somewhat eccentric. According to Wright, for example, the heart functions to pump blood because the heart pumps blood and the heart is present in the organism due to its pumping blood. More specifically, natural selection favoured animals with hearts by reason of their circulating blood (and not by reason of their making noise).

Is there reason to think that Searle is right about functions requiring values? Is there any reason to doubt that function can be understood in a wholly descriptive manner? Mark Bedau has argued that purely descriptive analyses are counterintuitive (1991; 1993). For example, Wright's analysis would imply that lifeless clay crystals have some functional features, since they are subject to a kind of natural selection. But it is very counterintuitive to say that a feature of a lifeless clay crystal has any function. Bedau further argues that, being counterintuitive, no purely descriptive analysis can be correct. The notion of value must be added to make such an analysis work. Bedau's view is similar to Searle's except that Bedau denies the fact/value dichotomy. In fact, he views the value element of functions as disproving it. However, Searle could still accept Bedau's intuitive appeals as supporting his view that functions require values.

There is an interesting similarity between Searle and Norman Malcolm (Malcolm, 1964). Both have argued that what looks like a scientific account of the mind, proposed by what appears to be a scientific vanguard, is actually incoherent. And each has done so by purportedly showing that a concept familiar from ordinary life or discourse is being misunderstood or misapplied by the self-styled vanguard. Their position is not even false, in other words. Malcolm tried to show that the essence of mental states, as determined by the semantics of mental predicates, is incompatible with the essence of brain states, as determined by the semantics of neural predicates. A similar argument has also been attributed to Max Black (Putnam, 1975, pp. 376–77). Some philosophers (Feyerabend, 1963; Hoffman, 1967; Churchland, 1986) have replied to Malcolm and Black by noting that one's concepts must change in order for there to be scientific advance. Albert Einstein, writing much earlier, evidently appreciated the point. Einstein's use of 'space' and 'time,' for example, are much further removed from experience and common sense than Newton's use.[4] 'Newton, forgive me; you found the only way which, in your age, was just about possible for a man of highest thought—and creative power. The concepts, which you created, are even today still guiding our thinking in physics, although we now know that they will have to be replaced by others farther removed from the sphere of immediate experience, if we aim at a profounder understanding of relationships' (Einstein, quoted in Hoffman, 1967, p. 129).

Taking one's cue from criticisms aimed at Black and Malcolm, the problem with Searle and Bedau's discussions is that they hold up our intuitive, prescientific folk concept of function as the analysandum for a theory of functions.[5] When Searle and Bedau discover that functions require values, they are revealing something about our old, pre-scientific concept of function. If one assumes a strict fact/value distinction, then Searle and (inadvertently) Bedau have shown that functions do not exist in unconscious nature, but this is only to show that an old, pre-scientific concept lacks an intrinsic application (cf. Bolender, 1998).[6]

---

[4] A more familiar illustration might be relativistic mass, but physicist Lev Okun argues that Einsteinian mass and Newtonian mass are the same (Okun, 1989).
[5] Mohan Matthen also faults Bedau on this point (1991).
[6] This is not to take sides as to which descriptive account of functions should be adopted. But it is to say that neither Searle nor Bedau has shown that some strictly descriptive approach *or other* is suitable for biological theorising.

Putnam criticised Feyerabend's view that scientific advance requires meaning change. Putnam noted that there are no clear criteria for meaning change, and so often there is no fact as to whether or not it has occurred (1975, pp. 432–33). But this doesn't do justice to the dialectic to which Feyerabend was contributing. He was making a concession to Malcolm and Black by assuming that there is a meaning change. If there are no clear criteria for meaning change, then it is Malcolm and Black who are undermined.[7] Likewise, if there are no clear criteria for meaning change with regard to the word 'function', then it is Searle who is undermined, not the cognitivist. If Putnam is right, the concept of *function* may not even be sharp enough for us to say whether or not functions require values. There may be no fact of the matter, just as there can be no fact of the matter as to whether a certain balding man is actually bald. In that case, the cognitivist has two options. One is to retain the word 'function' and specify that there are purely descriptive functions. Or one could invent a new term to express the more precise and purely descriptive concept. Nothing important turns on which decision is made.

Summary

Searle's argument for digital computation being observer-relative rather than intrinsic would, if it is sound, undermine the approach of this book. The computations underpinning relational cognition must be observer-independent for them to be a subject for science. But Searle's claim that any process is as digital as any other overlooks the objective basis for categorising certain processes as digital. There is a striking, and perfectly objective, contrast between, say, a neuron's pulsing versus a rock's just lying there on the ground.

---

[7] In all fairness to Putnam, he was not defending Malcolm or Black, and Feyerabend was sometimes quite liberal in interpreting a scientific advance as involving meaning change. But meaning change isn't strictly required for refuting Malcolm or Black, as Feyerabend sometimes acknowledged.

Digital computation also essentially involves following an algorithm, and part of Searle's attack on cogitivsm is an attempt to show that following an algorithm is impossible in the absence of a conscious observer. Algorithmic processes in biology can be distinguished from non-algorithmic ones by noting that the former function to arrive at their end states. Searle's insistence that functions themselves are observer-relative assumes a pre-scientific value-laden conception of functions, a conception which we are not required to adopt.

Chapter Six

Beyond the Infinite

Are there alternatives to a generative approach to a social-relational grammar? Are there alternatives to a generative approach to language? Consider the following: '[T]here is no motivation for any generative apparatus at all. An NL [natural language] grammar should, I believe, be regarded as an *axiom system* whose elements are statements to which truth values can be assigned, not as a sentence formation machine implementable as a computer program' (Postal, 2004, p. 110). In other words, Postal regards NL grammars as model-theoretic rather than proof-theoretic. Some considerations favouring model-theoretic grammars for natural languages may have analogues for relational cognition. The matter bears looking into.

Model-theoretic grammars are the same as what Geoffrey Pullum means by model-theoretic syntax; proof-theoretic grammars are the same as what he means by generative-enumerative syntax.

> MTS [model-theoretic syntax] rules are simply assertions about the structure of expressions. That is, an MTS rule makes a statement that is either true or false when evaluated in the structure of an expression. If a structure is to be grammatically well formed according to a certain rule, then the rule must be true as interpreted in that structure.
>
> Rules within GES [generative-enumerative syntax] are not like this. A GES rule is an instruction forming part of a procedure for stepwise construction of a derivation—a rule-mediated sequence of representations, the last of which is by definition well formed. Crucially, GES rules do not assert anything about the structure of well-formed expressions; they are instructions making up individual parts of an integrated procedure for building such struc-

tures, and they cannot be interpreted in isolation. (Pullum, 2007, p. 1, emphasis deleted)

Postal and Pullum, among others, have suggested that a model-theoretic grammar can do the same work as a proof-theoretic grammar. They claim that the bias in linguistics toward proof-theoretic grammars is an irrational prejudice. Hence, in explaining the astronomical number of sentences (and also mods?) that the mind can grasp, Merge should not be the default hypothesis, in their view.

> Claims that [generative] operations are '(virtually) conceptually necessary'/inevitable/inescapable/etc. are mere propaganda which cannot hide the fact that such operations have never been argued to serve any proper function in a linguistic theory. To show that they did, one would at the least need an argument that proof-theoretic grammars embodying operations (like Merge, Copy, various transformations, etc.) are superior to model-theoretically interpreted grammars consisting of statements… As far as I know, though, the literature is entirely free of any such argument. (Postal, 2003b, p. 609, emphasis deleted)

How might one replace a set-theoretic grammar, the sort of grammar proposed in Chapter Three, with an equally powerful model-theoretic grammar? The question is so abstract, it can be discussed without specifying whether we mean mods or sentences. For simplicity, assume a lexicon of one item: $\{\alpha\}$. With a set-constructive operation and $\{\alpha\}$, we have a recursive definition of an infinite set of sets. A recursive definition partly consists of a specification of an initial term, the base clause. In the present case, the base clause is $\{\alpha\}$. A recursive definition also includes a recursion clause, this being an algorithm for deriving a term from its predecessor. Let Merge-α be the recursion clause. Merge-α takes $\{x\}$ as input and produces $\{\alpha, \{x\}\}$ as output, for any x. This recursive definition is a set- theoretic grammar for generating an infinite number of hierarchically structured expressions beginning with $\{\alpha\}$, namely $\{\alpha\}$, $\{\alpha,\{\alpha\}\}$, $\{\alpha,\{\alpha,\{\alpha\}\}\}$, and so on. It is the recursive definition for this infinite set. Given the earlier characterisation of proof-theoretic grammars, any set-theoretic grammar is also proof-theoretic.

Hence the recursive definition for this infinite set is also a proof-theoretic grammar for the set.

Gottlob Frege showed that any recursive definition can be replaced with an explicit definition.[1] While a recursive definition is an operation for constructing the members of a collection, an explicit definition states conditions for membership in the collection. A model-theoretic grammar is an explicit definition. In principle, a set-theoretic grammar can be replaced with a model-theoretic grammar, but the question remains as to which approach is more plausible.

Considering how the replacement is possible may help us decide. The replacement is made possible by means of a relation known as 'the ancestral' (Frege, 2000, pp. 167–208; Quine, 1947; 1966). The concept of the ancestral makes it possible to explain the notion of following in a sequence. An ancestral is a transitive relation defined with regard to an intransitive relation. For example, the ancestral of the relation *parent of* is *ancestor of*. The ancestral of *offspring of* is *descendant of*. The ancestral of *immediate successor of* is *successor of*. The set recursively defined above is explicitly defined as the set whose members are $\{\alpha\}$ and all successors of $\{\alpha\}$.

On the face of it, the explicit definition is beautifully simple. But this initial impression is deceiving, since the definition requires a definition of the relevant ancestral which turns out to be complex. In fact, before defining the ancestral notion *successor of*, one also needs to define *immediate successor of*. As Frege observed, y immediately succeeds x if, and only if, there is a set F and an object z such that z is a member of F, y is the cardinal number of the set F (i.e. the number of members of F), and x is the cardinal number of the set {*object other than z belonging to F*}. Regarding natural

---

[1] The following discussion is based on a personal communication from Noam Chomsky, the most relevant part of which follows: 'Via the Fregean ancestral, any recursive operation can be replaced by a direct definition, in set-theoretic terms. It remains true that Merge is the simplest operation that yields an infinite array of hierarchically structured elements, whether one presents it in simplest form as an operation or complicates it in terms of a direct definition with an axiom system providing the relevant (elementary) set theory' (28.4.08).

numbers, 2 immediately succeeds 1. How is this relation to be explicitly defined? Let F be the set of planets whose orbits lie between Sun and Earth, and let z be Venus. 2 *immediately succeeds* 1 if, and only if, 2 is the cardinal number of the set {*planets whose orbits lie between Sun and Earth*}, and 1 is the cardinal number of the set {*object other than Venus belonging to F*}. Similarly, {α, {α}} immediately succeeds {α} if, and only if, the cardinal number of the set {*planets whose orbits lie between Sun and Earth*} is the number of occurrences of α in {α, {α}}, and the cardinal number of the set {*object other than Venus belonging to F*} is the number of occurrences of α in {α}.

How does one explicitly define *successor of* in terms of *immediate successor of*? We need first a definition of *closure*. Following Willard Quine (1947, p. 215), let '$R''y \subseteq y$' mean that whatever bears relation R to a member of set y is also a member of y. In other words, the set of things bearing relation R to any member of y is included in y. In yet other words, y is *closed with respect to R*. For example, the set of males is closed with respect to the relation of being a nephew, since any nephew of a male is also male. We simplify Frege's definition of *successor of* by stipulating, with Quine (1947; 1966, p. 46), that any object is a successor of itself. For example, one successor of {α} is {α}. As a definition, *the successors of* {α} are the common members of all sets containing {α} and all immediate successors of members. That is, z is a successor of {α} if, and only if, (for any set y) [((immediate successor of''$y \subseteq y$) & ({α}$\in$y))$\Rightarrow$($z \in y$)]. Given that *successor of* is the ancestral of *immediate successor of*, one here explicitly defines the ancestral closure of {α}.

The explicit definition requires the above definition of *successor of* which, in turn, requires the earlier definition of *immediate successor of* as well as definitions of such set-theoretic concepts as *membership*, *inclusion* and *closure*. The recursive definition, by contrast, is simply {α} and Merge-α. Between these two fundamentally different definitions of 'and so on', the recursive one seems much simpler. Given that simplicity is a consideration, there should be a bias toward a set-theoretic approach over a model-theoretic one, all else being equal.

There is another reason for considering a set-theoretic approach to be simpler than a model-theoretic one. A model-theoretic grammar alone, being merely a database, would be inert. We also need an operation to construct representations. One can see why by considering a parable by Fodor.

> Here is the way we tie our shoes:
> There is a little man who lives in one's head. The little man keeps a library. When one acts upon the intention to tie one's shoes, the little man fetches down a volume entitled *Tying One's Shoes*. The volume says such things as: 'Take the left free end of the shoelace in the left hand. Cross the left free end of the shoelace over the right free end of the shoelace..., etc.'
> When the little man reads the instruction 'take the left free end of the shoelace in the left hand', he pushes a button on a control panel. The button is marked 'take the left free end of a shoelace in the left hand'. When depressed, it activates a series of wheels, cogs, levers, and hydraulic mechanisms. As a causal consequence of the functioning of these mechanisms, one's left hand comes to seize the appropriate end of the shoelace. Similarly, *mutatis mutandis*, for the rest of the instructions.
> The instructions end with the word 'end'. When the little man reads the word 'end', he returns the book of instructions to his library.
> That is the way we tie our shoes. (Fodor, 1968, p. 627)

One finds here 'a finite set of operations with a fixed mode of application such that after a finite number of steps any element of the set to be characterised is specified', as Langendoen and Postal characterised proof-theoretic approaches (1984, p. 17). An element of the set is a tying of one's shoes. Fodor is quick to acknowledge how crude this account is. For one thing, it is not biological enough. The cogs and wheels will have to go, naturally. Further, as an unanalysed homunculus, the little man in the head is not acceptable. Instead, he must be understood as a committee of simpler mechanisms working in tandem. But these qualifications are irrelevant to current concerns. Let's just stick with the little man in the head.

Reflecting on this passage from Fodor, Stephen Stich and Ian Ravenscroft make an observation which is relevant to the debate about proof-theoretic versus model-theoretic approaches.

> In Fodor's account, the little man inside the head has a single book specifying a set of rules for accomplishing the task at hand. But we might also imagine that in some instances the little man has two books for a given ability. One of the books contains declarative sentences rather than rules. These might, for example, be a set of axioms for some branch of mathematics or science. Or they might be a set of principles detailing generalisations and more idiosyncratic facts in some other domain. Now, of course, axioms or generalisations or statements of fact cannot, by themselves, tell us how to do anything. That's the job of the second book, which is much the same as the book imagined in Fodor's shoe-tying example. It provides rules for using the information in the first book to accomplish some task. So, for example, if the first book contains statements of the laws in some branch of physics, the second book might contain rules which specify how to use these laws to solve physics problems. *Or perhaps the first book contains an axiomatic specification of all the sentences in a given language, and the second book contains a set of rules for using this specification efficiently in determining whether or not a given sentence is in the language.* (Stich and Ravenscroft, 1994, p. 455, emphasis added)

The passage reveals an ambiguity in the phrase 'model-theoretic account'. One could use the phrase to mean a one-book account for some given competence, the book being a list of axioms. Or one could use the phrase to mean a two-book account, namely a list of axioms plus a list of instructions. The latter is not purely model-theoretic, but a combined account. On the other hand, as Stich and Ravenscroft make clear, the former sort of account is not even coherent. The one-book account leaves the little man with no knowledge of how to do the thing in question, e.g. form a representation of a sentence, or form a representation of a complex mod. Hence, any one-book model-theoretic account is not an option.

A two-book approach is more complex than a one-book approach. If simplicity is a consideration, then a purely proof-theoretic account has an edge over a model-theoretic account. The former can get by with only one book, whereas the latter cannot. The point generalises, applying both to language and to mods.

To say that mods result from a set-theoretic grammar, however, is not to say that relational models as such result entirely from such a grammar. Recall that a relational model is not just a mod, but a mod conjoined with a preo. There are good reasons for thinking that model-theoretic grammars enter into relational cognition at some point, but not in mod building.

A proof-theoretic grammar for generating relational models would require that the total collection of relational models be recursively enumerable. This is because a proof-theoretic grammar for anything entails recursive enumerability. One can give a recursive definition of 'natural number', but one cannot give a recursive definition for 'real number'. This is because only countable collections can be recursively enumerated, and the collection of real numbers is not countable. So if the collection of relational models were uncountably infinite, there could be no proof-theoretic grammar for relational models. Likewise, the collection of plane figures which could occupy a continuous two-dimensional space could not be generated by a proof-theoretic grammar. This is because for any two-dimensional space, there is an uncountably infinite collection of possible plane figures which could occupy it.

> [T]here are at least two different kinds of infinity. The first, the infinity of the natural numbers (and of any equivalent sets), is called aleph nought ($\aleph_0$). Sets with cardinality $\aleph_0$ are called countable. The second kind of infinity is the one represented by a line segment. Its cardinality is designated by a lower-case German c (c), for 'continuum.' *Any* line segment, of arbitrary length, has cardinality c. So does any rectangle in the plane, any cube in space, or for that matter all unbounded n-dimensional space, whether n is 1, 2, 3 or 1,000. (Davis and Hersh, 1981, p. 224)

Relational models potentially incorporate all the figures which could occupy a two-dimensional space. Therefore, there are uncountably many of them. Note that the learned component of a model can partly be learned through observation. It can include images, sounds, and so forth. Not everything in a model needs to be verbalisable.

For example, an instance of Authority Ranking could contain the following rule: 'Only members of the highest class may wear the insignia ℘ at any time, and they must do so on state occasions.' Given that any volume of space, including a finite one, contains an uncountably infinite number of points, ℘ is only one of an uncountably infinite number of shapes that could figure into the model. To illustrate the point: one could imagine a ℘ morphing, in a continuous manner, within its two-dimensional space into a ℜ. If such a morphing were to occur, an uncountably infinite number of intermediate shapes would be realised in the process. Any one of them could enter into a social rule. Hence, there is an uncountably infinite collection of such potential rules. Given that such rules are potential components of models, then there is a uncountably infinite collection of possible models. But if the number of models is uncountably infinite, then the collection of models is not recursively enumerable. Given that it is not recursively enumerable, then the collection cannot be generated by a proof- theoretic grammar. The conclusion is that complex relational models are not specified by a proof-theoretic grammar alone. This is why the earlier discussion of Merge concerned the production of mods, not full-blown models. The collection of all preos is uncountable, since it includes shapes which are as vast in number as the points in a continuum.

Given that Merge best explains the digital infinity of mods, the collection of all mods is recursively enumerable and hence countably infinite. But preos include potentially uncountably infinitely many representations of shape. Hence, there are uncountably infinitely many potential preos. It is the preonic component that takes us beyond digital computation. Necessarily, an analogue system enters into the creation of preos. This is one reason why Braddon-Mitchell and Jackson's map account is plausible, for at least some mental capacities. ℘ and ℜ occupy two positions in a continuous map of possible shapes.

Preos would have to incorporate a model-theoretic component in order to include iconic elements, such as insignia and suchlike. Those preos which are rules could be understood as axioms in the model-theoretic sense. They characterise acceptable relational models by describing what such a model should be like.[2] But this does not mean that the proof- theoretic component of relational cognition can be discarded.

Given that a model-theoretic grammar must eventually be introduced anyway, have I begged the question in favour of a set-theoretic approach by discussing mods and preos separately? I do not believe that I have. The same mod can unite with various preos. This is an independent reason for distinguishing mods from preos. It is a reason for viewing them as being independently produced. Considered in isolation from preos, the mods exhibit digital infinity. The simplest explanation for this is that Merge serves as a mod-building operation. Further productivity enters in preonically.

We see now how appropriate it is that Fiske refers to relational models as 'models'. A model-theoretic grammar for social interaction consists of a set of relational models. However, one component of this system is proof-theoretic, namely the system for building mods. There is nothing very surprising about this, much less paradoxical. Sentences, evidently, result from a proof-theoretic system. But a sentence can serve as an axiom in a model-theoretic grammar. Likewise, a mod results from a proof-theoretic system. The mod is then conjoined with a preo (which itself may include sentences) to form a relational model. The relational model

---

[2] This is analogous to one of Postal's arguments for NL grammars being model theoretic (2004, Ch. 6). Postal notes that an iconic shape or sound can be a constituent in a sentence. There are uncountably many shapes and sounds, hence at least as many sentences. Cedric Boeckx (2006) has challenged Postal's argument by noting that, on the theory of late insertion (Halle and Marantz, 1993; 1994), Merge produces a complete structure prior to accessing any phonological features. This would mean that iconic elements are late comers arriving after the digital computation is completed. Nonetheless, the phenomenon that Postal draws attention to illustrates that there are analogue processes in language in addition to digital ones.

then serves in a model-theoretic grammar. The morality of a particular community, as internalised in an individual, would be such a model-theoretic grammar.

While on the topic of Turing computability, consider a possible objection to the claim that Merge is widely biologically realised. One could imagine someone objecting to the claim made earlier that fungi, mycelia, slime moulds and rangeomorphs exhibit digital infinity. The objection I have in mind takes the form of a dilemma. Either one idealises by subtracting performance limitations or one does not. If one does idealise, then these biological structures (fungi, etc.) are literally fractal; each is infinite. In fact, the number of iterations in a fractal constitutes a Cantor set. This means that the number of iterations in a fractal is uncountably infinite. An infinity of iterations, whether countable or uncountable, is not Turing computable. A Turing machine, you see, comes to a halt. Merge generates Turing computable sets. Since a complete fractal is not Turing computable, it is not generated by Merge. Therefore, Merge is not realised in fungi, etc.

That was one horn of the supposed dilemma. The other horn is that one chooses not to idealise. Each particular biological structure would then be finite. But then the collection of all such structures would itself be finite. There was, for example, only a finite number of rangeomorphs. Given that the universe will not carry on forever, and has not been forever, there is only a finite number of slime moulds. And so on. This would mean that these biological structures do not exhibit digital infinity by reason of not being infinite. Given either horn of the dilemma, there is no reason to posit Merge.

The trouble with the supposed dilemma is that it assumes that there is only one possible idealisation. It assumes that there is no reason to utilise an intermediate idealisation in order to focus attention on the infinite collection of all possible finitely recursive, say, slime moulds. In other words, we can generalise one size limitation from actual organisms (namely, each structure being finite) while refusing to generalise some other size limitation (namely, the finitude of the set of all actual slime moulds). But why would one want to focus attention on this relatively small but infinite collection? One reason is that it reveals a formal property shared across biological systems, including language, relational cognition and unbounded counting. This is also one possible reason for wanting to focus on the infinite collection of all possible finite sentences, i.e. to recognise digital infinity in language as well. One of the purposes of science is to discover unity across apparent diversity. That can be a motivation here too.

The motivation has, however, been criticised:

> I cannot stress this point too strongly — it is a fundamental issue in the study of pattern formation. When we see two things that look alike, our instinct is to attribute to them the same basic cause — to infer that at root they represent the same phenomenon... Our facility at recognizing and comparing patterns may help us to identify connections between systems that seem at face value to have no prospect of being related. But this mental faculty is apt to tempt us into making false correlations and untenable analogies. (Ball, 2009, p. 35)

This would be a good criticism of anyone thinking they can derive a solid conclusion simply by noticing similarities. But it is not a good criticism of someone devising an hypothesis to test. A knack for spotting similar patterns across cases can be very valuable in devising hypotheses which must then face the jury of empirical elimination.

Summary

The approach on offer here is proof-theoretic. Postal has argued that the bias in syntactic theory toward proof-theoretic grammars is irrational, and if his case is strong there should be an equally strong case against proof-theoretic approaches to relational cognition. Postal's point, evidently, is that for any empirically adequate proof-theoretic grammar there is an equally adequate model-theoretic grammar. But this observation does not address the question of simplicity. Would the model-theoretic grammar be as simple as the proof-theoretic one? There are two reasons to doubt that it would be. Since they utilise Merge, the proof-theoretic grammars in question are recursive definitions of sets of mental representations. Frege showed how, for any recursive definition, there is a corresponding explicit definition. In the case of either syntax or relational cognition, the explicit definition would be a model-theoretic grammar. But note that the explicit definition is considerably more complex than the corresponding recursive definition, given the complexity of defining the ancestral relation. Stich and Ravenscroft have also argued that no grammar can be purely model-theoretic. There must be a proof-theoretic component even for a model-theoretic approach, and so the model-theoretic approach ends up incorporating a proof-theoretic apparatus anyway. This is because a purely model-theoretic grammar would be nothing but a data base, a set of descriptions of well-formed representations. One still needs something to produce representations in the first place. Since a model-theoretic approach would combine a set of axioms with Merge anyway, it is *prima facie* simpler just to posit Merge.

Envoy

There are a number of reasons for positing a combinatorial system underlying interpersonal cognition. One is the wide variety of social interpretations, expectations and structures. This great diversity suggests the combination of objects rather than moving through spaces in the analogue manner. It stands in contrast, for example, to the blending of substances, which tends to average out differences rather than producing greater variety. Another reason for positing a combinatorial system is the systematicity of the complex relational models. In fact, systematicity virtually reveals transposable constituents of relational mental representations. Given that the mods exhibit digital infinity, specifically the digitally infinite use of finite means, there must be a set-constructive operation for generating this infinity. Hence, the digital infinity of the mods not only further supports the claim that a combinatorial procedure underlies interpersonal cognition but clarifies what sort of combinatorial procedure is in play.

Language, of course, also has the above-mentioned properties: diversity of sentence structures, systematicity, digitally infinite use of finite means. This raises the question of whether these features in interpersonal cognition are due to language. It is possible that they are, but there is nonetheless some evidence indicating that they are not. The recursive embedding of relational models is found in other species, such as baboons and dolphins. This raises the possibility that Merge in language and Merge in interpersonal cognition are multiple realisations of the same property. This is less surprising than Chomsky has suggested, given that digital infinity is not as biologically rare as he has supposed.

Formulating a universal grammar for interpersonal cognition is useful, because it defines precisely the possible mods. It provides an inventory of mods, in other words. This, in turn, is the first step in mapping mods onto brain states, a necessary step in devising a reduction of the computational core of interpersonal cognition to neuroscience.

Glossary

algorithm A finite step-by-step procedure for obtaining a result. Theoretically, the derivation of a sentence follows an algorithm, as does the construction of a compound *mod*.

analogue system Any system producing novelty by change of position within a continuous space. The continuous rotation of gears in the Antikythera mechanism, for example, means that there are continuum many possible outputs. (See *map story*.)

Authority Ranking The role played by ordered differences in relational cognition. Examples: military rankings, royal privilege and responsibility. (See *Relational Models Theory*.)

blending system Any system which mixes substances resulting in an averaging out of differences. Blending systems form a subclass of *analogue systems*. Blending systems stand in contrast to *particulate systems*.

cognitivism Roughly, the view that the brain is a digital computer. In this book, the term is also used more broadly to include the view that a given neural subsystem is a digital computer. Conceivably, one could be a cognitivist with regard to one neural subsystem while rejecting cognitivism with regard to another.

Communal Sharing The role played by having something in common in relational cognition. Examples: intense romantic love, racism, patriotism. (See *Relational Models Theory*.)

competence Knowledge, such as the knowledge of mods or knowledge of syntax. Contrasted with *performance*.

competence/performance distinction The distinction between knowledge (*competence*) and its implementation. For example, one may know the rules of multiplication, but one may not be able to perform a certain multiplication problem in one's head because it is too complicated. One could do so, however, if one's short-term memory were sufficiently extended. In other words, one has the knowledge needed to do all multiplication problems, but limitations on the system of implementation (*performance* limitations) make certain multiplications unfeasible.

compositional meaning The meaning of a mental representation seen as derivable from the meanings of its constituent representations and their arrangement. Widely believed to be a property of sentences, compound models in relational cognition also evidently exhibit compositional meaning.

contrary-to-fact conditional or **counterfactual conditional** How things would consequently be if some factor had been different or were different. Example: *If Germany had invaded Spain, then Germany would have won WWII* is a contrary-to-fact conditional which may or may not be true.

countable A collection is countable just in case its members can be placed in one-one relation with some subset of the natural numbers. Since there are infinite subsets of the set of natural numbers, there are countably infinite sets. (See *uncountably infinite*.)

Copy An operation for multiplying *tokens* of a given *type*.

digital (or **discrete**) **infinity** A *particulate system* exhibits digital infinity just in case there is no greatest number of times that its discrete units can be combined to form a compound object.

Equality Matching The role played by additive imbalances in relational cognition. Examples: turn taking; one person, one vote. (See *Relational Models Theory*.)

exaptation Any biological trait which is either a *spandrel* or a preadaptation, a preadaptation being a trait which serves a different function than the one for which it was first naturally selected.

fractal A geometrical pattern that is self-similar on every scale of magnification. Not all self-similarity is fractal, however. The pattern must be divisible into at least two fragments, each being a smaller version of the complete pattern. Example: the Sierpiński triangle.

Galilean idealisation Subtracting or ignoring details of a system which would result in computational or calculational intractability for the sake of devising a scientific explanation. (See *minimalist idealisation*.)

generative (See *generation*.)

generation Specifying how to construct a given structure, such as a compound *mod*.

idealisation (See *Galilean idealisation* and *minimalist idealisation*.)

interface The boundary between two mental faculties; the place where information between faculties is exchanged and their activities coordinated.

interpersonal cognition Same as *relational cognition*.

lexicon In linguistics, the lexicon is the reservoir of objects from which the computational core of grammar draws. In this book, the term is used broadly to mean any reservoir of objects upon which a computational system draws, e.g. the computational system which builds compound *mods*.

map story The view that cognition is an *analogue system* in the sense that it consists of change of position within at least one mentally represented map. On some versions of the map story, all cognition may be understood in this manner. On other versions, only certain forms of cognition fit this description.

Market Pricing The role played by ratios in *relational cognition*. Examples: maximising utility, determining the right monetary amount to reward an accomplishment. (See *Relational Models Theory*.)

Merge '[A] primitive operation that takes n objects already constructed and constructs from them a new object: in the simplest case, the set of these n objects... With Merge available, we instantly have an unbounded system of hierarchically structured expressions' (Chomsky, 2005, p. 11).

minimalist idealisation Subtracting or ignoring irrelevant details of a system for the sake of devising a scientific explanation. (See *Galilean idealisation*.)

model-theoretic system or **model-theoretic grammar** A finite characterisation of a non-finite collection (of sentences, mods, etc.). A model-theoretic system consists of descriptions of structures such that all and only members of the collection fit the descriptions. Contrasts with *proof-theoretic system*.

mods The *relational models* in their purely formal aspect considered apart from any semantic content or constraints on implementation. Fiske identifies mods with the elementary relational models (2004, pp. 58f). In this book, however, compound structures are also included as mods. (See *preos*.)

multiple realisation The occurrence of the same macro property in systems that are radically different on a micro level. The term usually appears in philosophy of mind, as in reference to multiply realised mental properties such as pain. But multiple realisation is conceptually close to *universality*, as noted by Batterman (2000).

particulate system   Any system which combines discrete objects to form compound structures. The objects do not change their intrinsic character upon combination. A particulate system has the capacity to increase the range of differences. Particulate systems stand in contrast to *blending systems* which tend to average out differences.

performance   The implementation of knowledge in action. Contrasted with *competence*.

Platonism   The view that there are entities without space–time location.

preonic systems   The systems responsible for supplying a semantic interpretation to a *mod* thus yielding a *relational model*.

preos   A *preo* is the semantic component of a *relational model*, in contrast to a *mod*.

primes   Elementary representations which combine to form complex representations.

proof-theoretic system or **proof-theoretic grammar**   A finite characterisation of a non-finite collection (of sentences, mods, etc.). A proof-theoretic system consists of constructive procedures such that applications of such procedures, in a finite number of steps, produce any given member of the collection. A *set-theoretic system* is a kind of proof-theoretic system. Contrasts with *model-theoretic system*.

recursion   The embedding of an object within an object of the same type. Example: a clause embedded in a clause.

recursive enumeration   The result of an *indefinitely recursive* procedure, a set whose members are *countably* infinite. I.e. they can be placed in one-one relation with the natural numbers. The full infinite output of a *Turing machine* is a recursive enumeration.

Relational Models Theory (RMT)   The theory that social structures are formed, motivated, and interpreted by means of four elementary mental models, namely *Communal Sharing*, *Authority Ranking*, *Equality Matching* and *Market Pricing*.

self-organisation   Change in a system which is not fully determined by external factors or genetically encoded instructions. Change arising internally in a system which is not fully encoded in advance.

set-theoretic system   A *proof-theoretic system* in which the constructive procedures generate sets. *Merge* is such a procedure.

Social Pattern Generator (SPG)   Hypothetically, a neural network producing different patterns of activity via *self-organisation*. Each pattern of activity corresponds to one of the elementary *mods*.

spandrel   A trait which is not directly the result of natural selection but proves to be useful. Example: the transparency of protein crystallins proved useful in the eye lens, but was already present in the lineage due to physics alone.

systematicity   The phenomenon in which the ability to have a certain thought virtually guarantees or highly probabilifies the ability to have a semantically close thought. For example, the ability to parse or understand *Henry spoke to James* practically guarantees the ability to parse or understand *James spoke to Henry*. Similarly, the ability to conceive of an instance of CS subordinated to an instance of MP, as in prostitution, practically guarantees the ability to conceive of an instance of MP subordinated to an instance of CS, as in a charitable organisation calculating how to maximise its effectiveness.

token   An occurrence of an entity. (See *type*.)

Turing machine A finite characterisation of a finite or infinite set. A Turing machine consists of 'a finite set of operations with a fixed mode of application such that after a finite number of steps any element of the set to be characterised is specified' (Langendoen and Postal, 1984, p. 17). Turing machines model digital computation. A typical digital computer, such as your laptop, is a Turing machine capable of imitating other Turing machines. By downloading a program to your laptop, you give it instructions for imitating some other Turing machine. (Named after the mathematician Alan Turing.)

type An entity abstracted from all actual and potential occurrences. 'In "John loves John," for example, there are three word-tokens but only two word-types' (Brody, 1967, p. 76). (See *token*.)

uncountably infinite A collection is uncountably infinite just in case its members do not stand in a one-one relation with any subset of the natural numbers. (See *recursive enumeration*.)

universality A formal property is universal just in case it appears in physically distinct systems. Example: the *critical exponent* β; '[T]he very *same* critical exponent β apparently describes the behavior of magnets as they undergo a transition from the ferromagnetic state with positive net magnetization below the critical point, to the paramagnetic phase with zero magnetiszation above the critical point' (Batterman, 2002a, p. 24). The book hypothesises that *digital infinity* exhibits universality in that it is both formal and can be instantiated in systems that are microstructurally quite different, such as the neural language faculty as well as pre-Cambrian rangeomorphs. It is hypothesised that universality is the same as *multiple realisation*.

Bibliography

Abler, W. (1989), 'On the particulate principle of self-diversifying systems', *Journal of Social and Biological Structures*, **12**, pp. 1–13.

Andley, U.P. (2006), 'Crystallins in the eye: Function and pathology', *Progress in Retinal and Eye Research*, **26**, pp. 78–98.

Aoun, J., Choueiri, L. and Hornstein, N. (2001), 'Resumption, movement, and derivational economy', *Linguistic Inquiry*, **32** (3), pp. 371–403.

Arthur, W.B. (2009), *The Nature of Technology: What It Is and How It Evolves* (London: Allen Lane).

Ball, P. (2009), *Branches: Volume III of Nature's Patterns* (Oxford: Oxford University Press).

Batterman, R.W. (1992), 'Explanatory instability', *Nous*, **26** (3), pp. 325–348.

Batterman, R.W. (2000), 'Multiple realizability and universality', *The British Journal for the Philosophy of Science*, **51**, pp. 115–145.

Batterman, R.W. (2002a), 'Asymptotics and the role of minimal models', *The British Journal for the Philosophy of Science*, **53**, pp. 21–38.

Batterman, R.W. (2002b), *The Devil in the Details: Asymptotic Reasoning in Explanation, Reduction, and Emergence* (Oxford and New York: Oxford University Press).

Baxter, R.J. (1982), *Exactly Solved Models in Statistical Mechanics* (London: Academic Press).

Bedau, M. (1991), 'Can biological teleology be naturalized?', *The Journal of Philosophy*, **88** (11), pp. 647–655.

Bedau, M. (1993), 'Naturalism and teleology', in *Naturalism: A Critical Appraisal*, eds. S. Wagner and S. Warner (Notre Dame: University of Notre Dame Press), pp. 23–51.

Bergman, T.J., Beehner, J.C., Cheney, D.L. and Seyfarth, R.M. (2003), 'Hierarchical classification by rank and kinship in baboons', *Science*, **302**, pp. 1234–1236.

Berlin, I. (1990), *The Crooked Timber of Humanity: Chapters in the History of Ideas*, ed. H. Hardy (London: Pimlico).

Berlin, I. (1998), 'My intellectual path', *The New York Review of Books*, **45** (8). Available on the internet:
[http://www.nybooks.com/articles/13853]. The in-text page reference is to the internet edition.

Bigelow, J. and Pargetter, R. (1987), 'Functions', *The Journal of Philosophy*, **84**, pp. 181–196.

Black, M. (1962), *Models and Metaphors* (Ithaca, NY: Cornell University Press).

Block, N. and Fodor, J. (1972), 'What psychological states are not', *Philosophical Review*, **81** (2), pp. 159–181.

Boden, M. (2006), *Mind as Machine: A History of Cognitive Science* (Oxford: Oxford University Press).

Boeckx, C. (2006), 'Review of *Skeptical Linguistic Essays*', *Journal of Linguistics*, **42**, pp. 216–221.

Boeckx, C. (2008), *Bare Syntax* (Oxford: Oxford University Press).

Boeckx, C. (2010), *Language in Cognition: Uncovering Mental Structures and the Rules Behind Them* (West Sussex: Wiley-Blackwell).

Bolender, J. (1998), 'Real algorithms: A defense of cognitivism', *Philosophical Inquiry*, **20**, pp. 41–58.

Bolender, J. (2001), 'A two-tiered cognitive architecture for moral reasoning', *Biology and Philosophy*, **16** (3), pp. 339–356.

Bolender, J. (2007a), 'Self-organization in the development of social cognition: Symmetry breaking and the relational-models framework', *Psychologia*, **5**, pp. 255–272.

Bolender, J. (2007b), 'Prehistoric cognition by description: A Russellian approach to the Upper Paleolithic', *Biology and Philosophy*, **22**, pp. 383–399.

Bolender, J. (2008), 'Hints of beauty in social cognition: Broken symmetries in mental dynamics', *New Ideas in Psychology*, **26**, pp. 1–22.

Bolender, J. (2010), *The Self-Organizing Social Mind* (Cambridge, MA, and London: MIT Press).

Braddon-Mitchell, D. and Jackson, F. (2007), *Philosophy of Mind and Cognition: An Introduction*, 2nd ed. (Malden, MA: Blackwell).

Brody, B.A. (1967), 'Glossary of logical terms', in *The Encyclopedia of Philosophy*, ed. P. Edwards (New York and London: Macmillan and The Free Press), pp. 57–77.

Carnie, A. (2007), *Syntax: A Generative Introduction*, 2nd ed. (Malden, MA: Blackwell).

Cartwright, N. (1989), *Nature's Capacities and Their Measurement* (Oxford: Clarendon).

Chomsky, N. (1965), *Aspects of the Theory of Syntax* (Cambridge, MA: MIT Press).

Chomsky, N. (1975), *The Logical Structure of Linguistic Theory* (Chicago, IL, and London: The University of Chicago Press).

Chomsky, N. (1988), *Language and Problems of Knowledge* (Cambridge, MA, and London: MIT Press).

Chomsky, N. (1995), *The Minimalist Program* (Cambridge, MA: MIT Press).

Chomsky, N. (2000a), *The Architecture of Language* (New Delhi: Oxford University Press).

Chomsky, N. (2000b), *New Horizons in the Study of Language and Mind* (Cambridge: Cambridge University Press).
Chomsky, N. (2003), 'Reply to Pietroski', in *Chomsky and His Critics*, eds. L.M. Antony and N. Hornstein (Oxford: Blackwell), pp. 304–307.
Chomsky, N. (2004, Jan.), 'On terrorism: Noam Chomsky interviewed by John Bolender', *JumpArts Journal*.
Chomsky, N. (2005), 'Three factors in language design', *Linguistic Inquiry*, **36** (1), pp. 1–22.
Chomsky, N. (2006), *Language and Mind*, 3rd ed. (Cambridge: Cambridge University Press).
Churchland, P.S. (1986), *Neurophilosophy* (Cambridge, MA: MIT Press).
Connor, R.C. (2007), 'Dolphin social intelligence: Complex alliance relationships in bottlenose dolphins and a consideration of selective environments for extreme brain size evolution in mammals', *Philosophical Transactions of the Royal Society B*, **362**, pp. 587–602.
Cummins, R. (1975), 'Functional analysis', *The Journal of Philosophy*, **72** (20), pp. 741–765.
Davis, P.J. and Hersh, R. (1981), *The Mathematical Experience* (Boston, MA: Birkhäuser).
Dawkins, R. (1986), *The Blind Watchmaker: Why the Evidence of Evolution Reveals a Universe without Design* (New York: Norton).
Dennett, D.C. (1987), *The Intentional Stance* (Cambridge, MA, and London: MIT Press).
Dennett, D.C. (1995), *Darwin's Dangerous Idea* (New York: Simon & Schuster).
Evans, N. and Levinson, S.C. (2009), 'Authors' response', *Behavioral and Brain Sciences*, **32** (5), pp. 472–492.
Feyerabend, P.K. (1963), 'Materialism and the mind–body problem', *The Review of Metaphysics*, **17**, pp. 49–66.
Fisher, R.A. (1958), *The Genetical Theory of Natural Selection* (New York: Dover). First published in 1930.
Fiske, A.P. (1990), 'Relativity within Moose ('Mossi') culture: Four incommensurable models for social relationships', *Ethos*, **18**, pp. 180–204.
Fiske, A.P. (1991), *Structures of Social Life: The Four Elementary Forms of Human Relations* (New York: The Free Press).
Fiske, A.P. (1993), 'Social errors in four cultures: Evidence about universal forms of social relations', *Journal of Cross-Cultural Psychology*, **24**, pp. 463–494.
Fiske, A.P. (2004), 'Relational models theory 2.0', in *Relational Models Theory: A Contemporary Overview*, ed. N. Haslam (Mahwah, NJ: Lawrence Erlbaum Associates), pp. 3–25.
Fiske, A.P. (forthcoming), 'Foundations of social relations: Endogenous relational psychology and cultural transmission', *Perspectives in Psychological Science*.

Fiske, A.P. and Ehrenhalt, A. (n.d.), 'Basic relationships', *The Relational-Models Website*, [http://www.rmt.ucla.edu/]; accessed February 2010.

Fiske, A.P., Haslam, N. and Fiske, S.T. (1991), 'Confusing one person with another: What errors reveal about the elementary forms of social relations', *Journal of Personality and Social Psychology*, **60**, pp. 656–674.

Fodor, J.A. (1968), 'The appeal to tacit knowledge in psychological explanation', *The Journal of Philosophy*, **65** (20), pp. 627–640.

Fodor, J.A. (1988), *Psychosemantics* (Cambridge, MA: MIT Press).

Fodor, J.A. (2003), *Hume Variations* (Oxford: Oxford University Press).

Frege, G. (2000), *Conceptual Notation and Related Articles*, ed. and trans. T.W. Bynum (Oxford and New York: Oxford University Press).

Frisch, K. von. (1967), *The Dance Language and Orientation of Bees* (Cambridge, MA: Harvard University Press).

Fujikawa, H. and Matsushita, M. (1989), 'Fractal growth of *bacillus subtilis* on agar plates', *Journal of the Physical Society of Japan*, **58** (11), pp. 3875–3878.

Gentner, T.Q., Fenn, K.M., Margoliash, D. and Nusbaum, H.C. (2006), 'Recursive syntactic pattern learning by songbirds', *Nature*, **440** (7088), pp. 1204–1207.

Golinski, M.R., Boecklen, W.J. and Dawe, A.L. (2008), 'Two-dimensional fractal growth properties of the filamentous fungus *Cryphonectria parasitica*: The effects of hypovirus infection', *Journal of Basic Microbiology*, **48**, pp. 426–429.

Gould, S.J. (2002), *The Structure of Evolutionary Theory* (Cambridge, MA and London: Belknap Press).

Grice, H.P. (1969), 'Utterer's meaning and intentions', *Philosophical Review*, **78**, pp. 147–177.

Halle, M. and Marantz, A. (1993), 'Distributed morphology and the pieces of inflection', in *The View from Building 20*, eds. K. Hale and S.J. Keyser (Cambridge, MA: MIT Press).

Halle, M. and Marantz, A. (1994), 'Some key features of distributed morphology', *MIT Working Papers in Linguistics*, **21**, pp. 275–288.

Hargittai, I. and Hargittai, M. (2000), *In Our Own Image: Personal Symmetry in Discovery* (New York: Kluwer Academic/Plenum).

Harman, G. (2000), *Explaining Value and Other Essays in Moral Psychology* (Oxford: Oxford University Press).

Harris, Z. (1957), 'Co-occurrence and transformation in linguistic structure', *Language*, **33**, pp. 283–340.

Haslam, N. (ed.) (2004a), *Relational Models Theory: A Contemporary Overview* (Mahwah, NJ and London: Lawrence Erlbaum Associates).

Haslam, N. (2004b), 'A relational approach to the personality disorders', in *Relational Models Theory: A Contemporary Overview* (Mahwah, NJ: Lawrence Erlbaum Associates), pp. 335–362.

Haslam, N. (2004c), 'Research on the relational models: An overview', in *Relational Models Theory: A Contemporary Overview* (Mahwah, NJ: Lawrence Erlbaum Associates), pp. 27-57.

Haslam, N. and Fiske, A.P. (1992), 'Implicit relationship prototypes: Investigating five theories of the cognitive organisation of social relationships', *Journal of Experimental Social Psychology*, **28** (5), pp. 441-474.

Haslam, H., Reichert, T. and Fiske, A.P. (2002), 'Aberrant social relations in the personality disorders', *Psychology and Psychotherapy: Theory, Research and Practice*, **75**, pp. 19-31.

Hauser, M.D. (2006), *Moral Minds: How Nature Designed Our Universal Sense of Right and Wrong* (New York: Ecco).

Hauser, M.D., Chomsky, N. and Fitch, W.T. (2002), 'The faculty of language: What is it, who has it, and how did it evolve?', *Science*, **298**, pp. 1569-1579.

Hempel, C. (1965), *Aspects of Scientific Explanation* (New York: The Free Press).

Hoffman, R. (1967), 'Malcolm and Smart on brain-mind identity', *Philosophy*, **42** (160), pp. 128-136.

Honderich, T. (2004), *On Consciousness* (Edinburgh: Edinburgh University Press).

International Human Genome Sequencing Consortium (2001), 'Initial sequencing and analysis of the human genome', *Nature*, **409** (6822), pp. 860-921.

International Human Genome Sequencing Consortium (2004), 'Finishing the euchromatic sequence of the human genome', *Nature*, **431** (7011), pp. 931-945.

Jackson, F. and Pettit, P. (1988), 'Functionalism and broad content', *Mind*, **97** (387), pp. 381-400.

Jackson, F. and Pettit, P. (1992), 'In defense of explanatory ecumenism', *Economics and Philosophy*, **8**, pp. 1-21.

Janeway, C.A. (1993), 'How the immune system recognizes invaders', *Scientific American*, **269**, pp. 40-47.

Kohonen, T. (2001) *Self-Organizing Maps*, 3rd ed. (Berlin: Springer).

Langendoen, D.T. and Postal, P.M. (1984), *The Vastness of Natural Languages* (Oxford and New York: Blackwell).

Leary, T. (1957), *The Interpersonal Diagnosis of Personality: A Functional Theory and Methodology for Personality Evaluation* (New York: The Ronald Press).

Malcolm, N. (1964), 'Scientific materialism and the identity theory', *Dialogue*, **3** (2), pp. 115-125.

Matthen, M. (1991), 'Naturalism and teleology', *The Journal of Philosophy*, **88** (11), pp. 656-657.

Matsuyama, T. and Matsushita, M. (1993), 'Fractal morphogenesis by a bacterial cell population', *Critical Reviews in Microbiology*, **19** (2), pp. 117-135.

Mikhail, J. (2007), 'Universal moral grammar: Theory, evidence and the future', *Trends in Cognitive Sciences*, **11** (4), pp. 143-152.

Moskowitz, G.B. (2004), *Social Cognition: Understanding Self and Others* (New York: Guilford Press).
Nagel, E. (1977), 'Teleology revisited', *The Journal of Philosophy*, **74**, pp. 261–301.
Nagel, E. (1979), *The Structure of Science* (Indianapolis, IN, and Cambridge: Hackett).
Narbonne, G.M. (2004), 'Modular construction of early Ediacaran complex life forms', *Science*, **305** (5687), pp. 1141–1144.
Nietzsche, F. (1984), *Human, All Too Human*, trans. M. Faber with S. Lehmann (Lincoln, NE: University of Nebraska Press).
Nietzsche, F. (1994), *On the Genealogy of Morality*, ed. K. Ansell-Pearson, trans. C. Diethe (Cambridge: Cambridge University Press).
O'Donoghue, J. (2007), 'Ediacarans: The "long fuse" of the Cambrian explosion?', *New Scientist*, **194** (2599), pp. 34–38. Title of the print version: 'Life's long fuse.'
Okun, L.B. (1989), 'The concept of mass', *Physics Today*, **42** (6), pp. 31–36.
Paulhus, D.L. (2001), 'Normal narcissism: Two minimalist accounts', *Psychological Inquiry*, **12** (4), pp. 228–230.
Pannekoek, A. (2003), *Worker's Councils* (Edinburgh: AK Press).
Peitgen, H-O., Jürgen, H. and Saupe, D. (2004), *Chaos and Fractals: New Frontiers of Science*, 2nd ed. (New York: Springer).
Pierce, B.A. (2008), *Genetics: A Conceptual Approach*, 3rd ed. (New York: W.H. Freeman).
Pinker, S. (1995), *The Language Instinct* (New York: Harper Perennial).
Postal, P.M. (2003a), 'Remarks on the foundations of linguistics', *Philosophical Forum*, **34** (3–4), pp. 233–251.
Postal, P.M. (2003b), '(Virtually) conceptually necessary', *The Journal of Linguistics*, **39**, pp. 599–620.
Postal, P.M. (2004), *Skeptical Linguistic Essays* (Oxford: Oxford University Press).
Postal, P.M. (2009), 'The incoherence of Chomsky's "biolinguistic" ontology', *Biolinguistics*, **3** (1), pp. 104–123.
Pullum, G.K. (2007), 'The evolution of model-theoretic frameworks in linguistics', in *Model-Theoretic Syntax at 10* (proceedings of the MTS@10 workshop, August 13–17, organized as part of ESSLLI 2007, the European Summer School on Logic, Language and Information) eds. J. Rogers and S. Kepser (Dublin: Trinity College Dublin), pp. 1–10.
Putnam, H. (1975), *Mind, Language and Reality: Philosophical Papers, Volume 2* (Cambridge: Cambridge University Press).
Putnam, H. (1997), 'Functionalism: Cognitive science or science fiction?', In *The Future of the Cognitive Revolution*, eds D.M. Johnson and C.E. Erneling (Oxford & New York: Oxford University Press), pp. 32–44.
Putnam, H. (2002), *The Collapse of the Fact/Value Dichotomy, and Other Essays* (Cambridge, MA, and London: Harvard University Press).

Quine, W.V. (1947), *Mathematical Logic* (Cambridge, MA: Harvard University Press).
Quine, W.V. (1966), *Selected Logic Papers* (New York: Random House).
Radford, A. (1997), *Syntax: A Minimalist Introduction* (Cambridge: Cambridge University Press).
Roedder, E. and Harman, G. (2010) 'Linguistics and moral theory', in *The Moral Psychology Handbook*, ed. J.M. Doris (Oxford: Oxford University Press).
Russell, B. (1996), *Power: A New Social Analysis* (London and New York: Routledge).
Sampson, G. (2002), *Empirical Linguistics* (London and New York: Continuum).
Searle, J. (1992), *The Rediscovery of the Mind* (Cambridge, MA: MIT Press).
Simon, H.A. (1962), 'The architecture of complexity', *Proceedings of the American Philosophical Society*, **106** (6), pp. 467–482.
Smolensky, P. and Dupoux, E. (2009), 'Universals in cognitive theories of language', *Behavioral and Brain Sciences*, **32** (5), pp. 468–469.
Spelke, E.S. (2003), 'What makes us smart?: Core knowledge and natural language', in *Language in Mind: Advances in the Study of Language and Thought*, eds. D. Gentner and S. Goldin-Meadow (Cambridge, MA, and London: MIT Press), pp. 277–311.
Stewart, I. and Golubitsky, M. (1992), *Fearful Symmetry: Is God a Geometer?* (London: Penguin).
Stich, S. and Ravenscroft, I. (1994), 'What *is* folk psychology?', *Cognition*, **50**, pp. 447–468.
Strevens, M. (2008), *Depth: An Account of Scientific Explanation* (Cambridge, MA, and London: Harvard University Press).
Thompson, D.W. (1942), *On Growth and Form* (Cambridge: Cambridge University Press).
Turing, A.M. (1950), 'Computing machinery and intelligence', *Mind*, **59** (236), pp. 433–460.
van Gelder, T. (1995), 'What might cognition be, if not computation?', *The Journal of Philosophy*, **91** (7), pp. 345–381.
van Gelder, T. and Port, R.F. (1995), 'It's about time: An overview of the dynamical approach to cognition', in *Mind as Motion: Explorations in the Dynamics of Cognition*, eds. R.F. Port and T. van Gelder (Cambridge, MA: MIT Press), pp. 1–43.
Varley, R.A., Klessinger, N.J.C., Romanowski, C.A.J. and Siegal, M. (2005), 'Agrammatic but numerate', *Proceedings of the National Academy of Sciences of the United States of America*, **102** (9), pp. 3519–3524.
Wegner, D.M. and Vallacher, R.R. (1977), *Implicit Psychology: An Introduction to Social Cognition* (New York: Oxford University Press).
Weisberg, M. (2007), 'Three kinds of idealization', *The Journal of Philosophy*, **104**, pp. 639–659.

Wiggins, J.S. (1979), 'A psychological taxonomy of trait-descriptive terms: The interpersonal domain', *Journal of Personality and Social Psychology*, **37**, pp. 395–412.

Worchel, S., Cooper, J. and Goethals, G.R. (1989), *Understanding Social Psychology*, 4th edition (Pacific Grove, CA: Brooks/Cole).

Wright, L. (1973), 'Functions', *The Philosophical Review*, **82** (2), pp. 139–168.